04464017

D1625706

THE ANIMAL BOOK

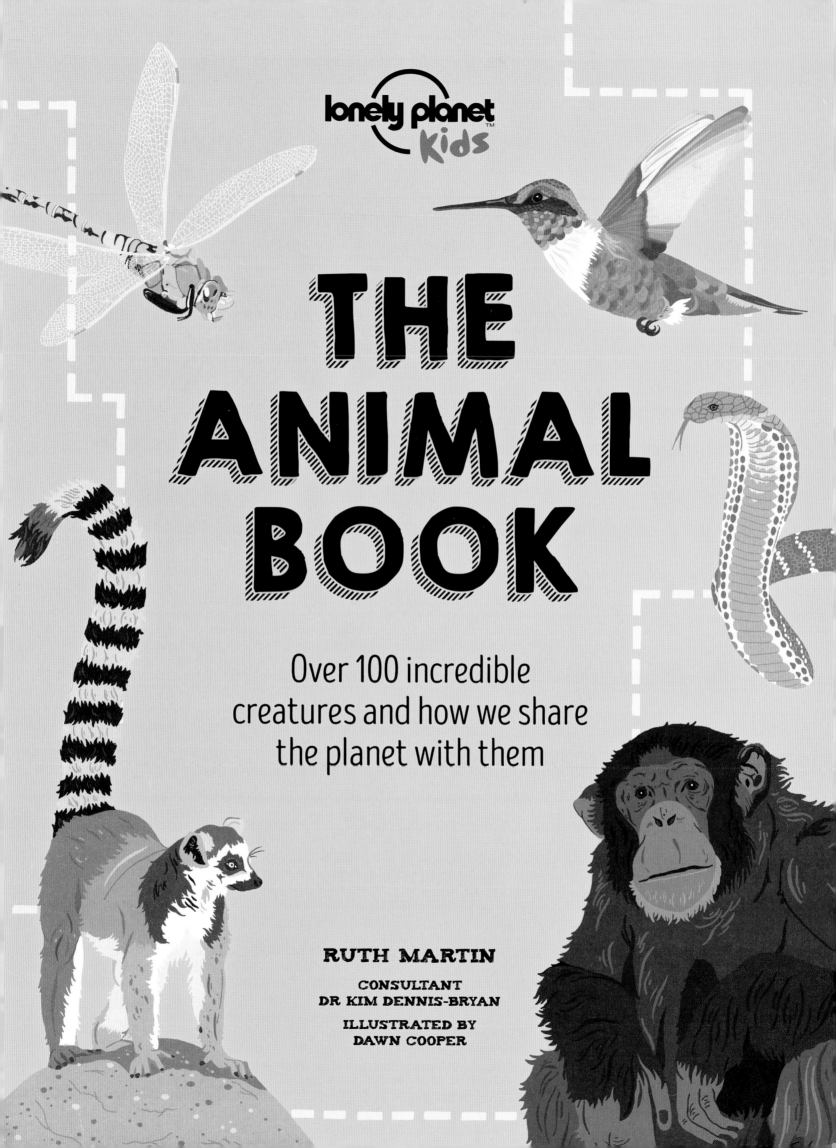

THE ANIMAL BOOK

Over 100 incredible
creatures and how we share
the planet with them

RUTH MARTIN

CONSULTANT
DR KIM DENNIS-BRYAN

ILLUSTRATED BY
DAWN COOPER

CONTENTS

THE KEY FACTS BOXES

Each animal in this book has a Key Facts box showing important details about the creature.

Scientific name:
Used by scientists, this is a unique name that gives the genus and species name of the creature. Where there is a third part to the name, it describes the subspecies.

Status:
This category is given by the International Union for Conservation of Nature (IUCN) based on how threatened or secure the animal is.

KEY FACTS

Scientific name: *Panthera tigris tigris*
Size: Head and body length: up to 2.9m; tail length: up to 1.1m
Diet: Mostly deer and pigs, occasionally animals as large as a gaur (Indian bison)

Status: Endangered (population decreasing)
Amazing fact: There are now only around 2,300 Bengal tigers in Asia, living in small populations of less than 250 each.

STATUS	MEANING
Extinct	The animal is believed to have died out completely.
Extinct in the wild	The animal is known to survive only in captivity or well outside its natural range.
Critically endangered	The animal faces an <u>extremely high risk</u> of becoming extinct in the wild. This status is determined by particular factors, including drops in population or threats to natural habitat.
Endangered	The animal faces a <u>very high risk</u> of extinction in the wild.
Vulnerable	The animal faces a <u>high risk</u> of extinction in the wild.
Near threatened	The animal is close to facing the threat of extinction in the near future.
Least concern	The animal is widespread or not currently at risk.
Data deficient	There is not enough information about the animal's risk of extinction.
Not evaluated	The animal has not yet been assessed.

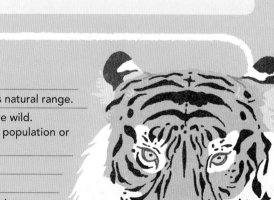

EARTH: PLANET OF LIFE

Earth is around 4.5 billion years old, but modern humans have lived here for only about 200,000 years. The planet does not belong to us; we share it with many other forms of life. So far, we have identified about 1.2 million species, and scientists think there may be around 8.7 million in total, although estimates vary wildly.

Explore this book to meet some of the most fascinating creatures from around the globe and discover the amazing ways we interact with them.

Enjoy the journey!

RUTH MARTIN - AUTHOR

Arctic Ocean

EUROPE

North Pacific Ocean

NORTH & CENTRAL AMERICA

North Atlantic Ocean

AFRICA

Indian Ocean

SOUTH AMERICA

South Atlantic Ocean

ARCTIC

PLANET EARTH

ANTARCTICA

ORDERS AND BORDERS

To help us understand the physical world, we divide land into cities, countries, regions and continents. This book is divided into chapters by continent or region. Some animals are found in several regions or worldwide, while others are limited to small areas and the most endangered may have just one protected location as their home.

ARRIVALS AND DEPARTURES

To help us understand the animal world, we team up similar animals into broader groups. Each kind of animal is part of a species, a genus, a family, an order, a class, a phylum, a kingdom and a domain. As time passes, the world changes and some animals, such as the dinosaurs, become extinct. Today, the main threat to animal survival is human activity. We also discover new creatures, adding to our knowledge of the animal kingdom. Currently, more than 10,000 new species are being discovered every year.

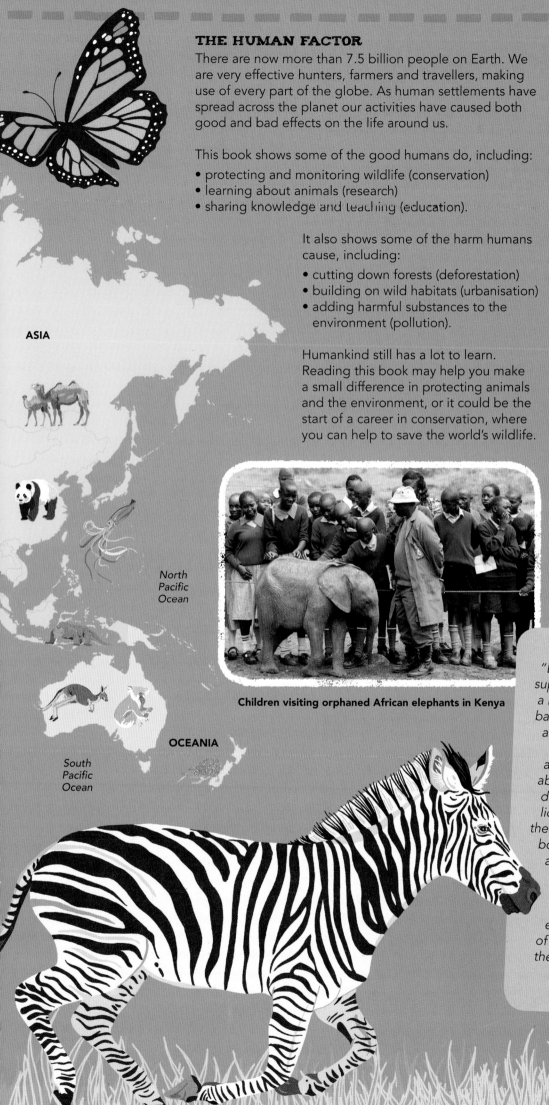

THE HUMAN FACTOR

There are now more than 7.5 billion people on Earth. We are very effective hunters, farmers and travellers, making use of every part of the globe. As human settlements have spread across the planet our activities have caused both good and bad effects on the life around us.

This book shows some of the good humans do, including:
• protecting and monitoring wildlife (conservation)
• learning about animals (research)
• sharing knowledge and teaching (education).

It also shows some of the harm humans cause, including:
• cutting down forests (deforestation)
• building on wild habitats (urbanisation)
• adding harmful substances to the environment (pollution).

Humankind still has a lot to learn. Reading this book may help you make a small difference in protecting animals and the environment, or it could be the start of a career in conservation, where you can help to save the world's wildlife.

ASIA

North Pacific Ocean

OCEANIA

South Pacific Ocean

Children visiting orphaned African elephants in Kenya

ZOOLOGIST DR KIM DENNIS-BRYAN

This book has been created with expert guidance from Kim Dennis-Bryan, Doctor of Zoology. Kim studied life sciences at university before obtaining her doctorate in zoology while researching at the Natural History Museum in London. She is a freelance writer and consultant as well as an Associate Lecturer with the Open University. Kim has been a Scientific Fellow of the Zoological Society in London for many years and is a Life Member of the Rare Breeds Survival Trust.

A WORD FROM KIM

"Earth is the only planet known to support life in huge numbers and in a multitude of forms, ranging from bacteria and plants to animals such as starfish, zebras and ourselves. Animals are remarkable – we are still learning amazing things about them, but many are rapidly disappearing. Elephants, rhinos, lions and tigers will be extinct in the wild before most readers of this book reach their mid-20s, unless attitudes change. Lesser-known animals such as corals and pangolins are also under threat. These creatures and their ecosystems are an essential part of our future. Only by conserving them will that future exist for the next generations to enjoy."

ARCTIC

The icy Arctic, at the very top of the world, plays a vital part in how the planet works. It lies between the northernmost point on Earth – the North Pole – and the Arctic Circle, an imaginary line that rings the top of the globe. The region is made up of the Arctic Ocean and the land that surrounds it, including parts of Canada, the U.S.A., Greenland, Norway, Finland, Sweden, Iceland and Russia. Home to a fascinating variety of wildlife and millions of people too, the Arctic is a winter wonderland full of surprises.

A MELTING OCEAN

Temperatures in the Arctic can drop below -50°C (-58°F) in winter, with a much warmer average of 0°C (-32°F) in summer. Part of the Arctic Ocean is covered in a layer of sea ice, stretching for millions of square kilometres. This giant white ice sheet reflects sunlight back into space, helping to keep the world cool. But our climate is warming and the ice is melting. Forecasts show that by 2100, the Arctic may have no sea ice at all in summer.

Map labels: Alaska (U.S.A.), Canada, ARCTIC OCEAN, North Pole, Greenland (Denmark), Svalbard (Norway), Norway, Finland, Sweden, Russia, ARCTIC CIRCLE

LIFE IN THE ARCTIC

The snowy conditions of the Arctic are just right for many well-adapted animals, including polar bears, walruses, seals and many others. As well as the wildlife, around four million people live in the Arctic. There are several groups of native inhabitants, such as the Inuit and Yupik people, who have built a rich culture in this challenging but beautiful place.

A WARMING WORLD

Our Earth is warming at an alarming rate. Each year, the sea ice around the North Pole is shrinking. Waste gases from human activity such as from vehicles, factories and power stations trap the Sun's heat in our atmosphere, causing the world to warm up like a greenhouse.

HUSKY

These intelligent dogs are known for their strength and speed in pulling sleds across the snow. Arctic communities, including the Inuit and the Yupik, have relied on dog sleds for their livelihoods. Today, there are separate breeds of sled dog, including the Siberian husky, the Eskimo dog and the Alaskan Malamute.

Huskies were originally bred to be working sled dogs, so as pets they need lots of exercise.

MUSHING
Dog racing, or 'mushing', is the state sport of Alaska, where huskies can reach speeds of around 31km per hour (19mi). They have the strength and stamina to race for three days over freezing ground, with a driver or 'musher' steering the pack.

DOUBLE THE FUR
Resembling wolves, huskies have two layers of dense fur to keep them warm. The coarse outer coat keeps them dry and the thick, woolly undercoat keeps them warm.

HERO HUSKIES
Huskies have helped on important tasks ranging from Antarctic expeditions in the 1800s to U.S. Army missions during World War II. They proved their hardy reputation in the Great Race of Mercy in 1925. During an outbreak of diphtheria, teams of huskies delivered a life-saving serum to the remote town of Nome. In a relay journey of nearly 1,127km (700 mi), 20 mushers delivered the cure in six days.

Balto, a Siberian husky, led his team on two stretches of the journey without a break. He is honoured as a national hero with his own statue in New York's Central Park.

KEY FACTS

Scientific name: *Canis familiaris*
Height: Up to 60cm at shoulder
Diet: Meat – working huskies often eat seal meat, while pets eat canned or dried food

Status: Domestic animal, not evaluated
Amazing fact: Huskies don't bark very much, but they will often howl like wolves.

REINDEER

Famous for pulling Santa's sleigh every Christmas, these strong creatures are also very important to other Arctic dwellers. There are many different names for reindeer in different cultures. In North America, they are generally known as caribou, while the Inuit people call them *tuku*.

While they grow, reindeer antlers have a velvety covering. When the antlers are fully grown, the 'velvet' is shed and rubs away.

REINDEER RIDES

Reindeer are hardworking creatures, strong enough to pull sleds filled with goods or supplies. Some Siberian reindeer owners ride them, while others farm thousands of them for meat and fur.

REINDEER ON THE MENU

In the region of northern Europe known as Lapland, reindeer meat makes a popular dish, either fresh or cured, often served as meatballs or sausages. There are also a few remaining nomadic communities, such as the Dukha people of Mongolia, who herd reindeer for milk, cheese and yoghurt.

In the wild, some reindeer make long migrations, with thousands of animals moving vast distances as the seasons change.

SÁMI REINDEER HERDERS

Reindeer herding is a very important part of the livelihood of the native Sámi people of Scandinavia. To protect their culture, laws now exist to ensure that only people from Sámi families can keep reindeer in some areas.

HO!
HO!
HO!

SANTA'S ON HIS WAY!

Can you name Santa's eight reindeer? The poem *A Visit from St. Nicholas* by Clement Clarke Moore (1823) names them Dasher, Dancer, Prancer, Vixen, Comet, Cupid, Dunder and Blixem (often called Donner and Blitzen). Did you say Rudolph? The famous 'Red-Nosed Reindeer' appeared later, in 1939, in a poem by Robert L. May.

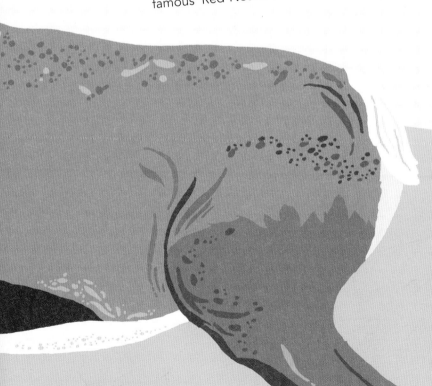

HERALDIC BEASTS

Reindeer are popular symbols in coats of arms, with many Nordic countries choosing to use them in heraldry to symbolize inner strength and the ability to survive in harsh environments.

KEY FACTS

Scientific name: *Rangifer tarandus*
Size: Height at shoulder: up to 1.4m; head and body length: up to 2.1m
Diet: Lichens, mosses, ferns, grasses, and the leaves and shoots of trees and shrubs

Status: Least concern (population stable)
Amazing fact: In most species of deer, only the male grows antlers, but in reindeer many females do too. The females' antlers are smaller than the males', and they shed them at different times of year.

HARP SEAL

Strong, sleek swimmers that roam the cold waters of the Arctic, harp seals spend most of their time at sea, in coastal waters near pack ice. They rely on the pack ice as a place to breed, and they gather in huge numbers during the breeding season, with as many as 2,000 animals per square kilometre (about 5,100 per sq mi). Harp seal pups have a soft white coat that has made them very valuable to the fur trade. Seal hunting is now controlled, but climate change brings new threats.

FROM FLUFFY TO FAST

Harp seal pups have soft white fur, called lanugo, which keeps them warm. By about 18 days old, this fur has moulted, to be replaced by a silvery coat. As adults, they have a streamlined body with thick blubber for warmth and strong hind flippers to propel them through icy waters.

RAIDING THE ROOKERIES

Seal meat was vital for the native people of the Arctic. They also traded seal fur, called pelts, but in limited numbers that did not harm the seal population. In the 19th century, fur became very popular. Soon European hunters tracked down 'rookeries', or breeding areas. Young seals were easy to catch, so the hunters killed them in great numbers.

Marine biologists monitor the health of seal pups.

CHANGING DANGERS

Laws now limit seal hunting and there are about nine million harp seals worldwide, producing over a million pups a year. These are healthy numbers, but global warming threatens their habitat. Harp seal pups cannot swim at first, so they rely on the sea ice. Warmer waters and melting ice put them at great risk.

KEY FACTS

Scientific name: *Pagophilus groenlandicus*
Size: Length: up to 1.7m
Diet: Fish and invertebrates, including Arctic cod and krill
Status: Least concern (population increasing)

Amazing fact: Harp seals spend most of their time in the open ocean. Some will swim up to 8,000km each year. They travel north in the summer, then south in the winter to return to their breeding grounds.

NARWHAL

With a striking spiral tusk and mottled skin, it is clear why this whale is known as the unicorn of the sea. Appearing from the depths, with its sword-like tusk, it has a mysterious quality that has inspired many legends and folklore tales.

LONG IN THE TOOTH

Male narwhals grow a long tusk – a spiralling tooth from the left side of the upper jaw. The purpose of the tusk is not completely clear. Packed with millions of nerve endings, it may be used to gather information from the water, or perhaps as a way for males to compare their strength.

HUNTING THE HORN

When the Inuit kill a narwhal, every part of the creature serves a purpose, from the skin and blubber, which are eaten, to the bones and tusk used for tools and crafts. Others hunt narwhals less respectfully, for their tusks alone, which can be worth thousands of dollars. Because they can be particularly difficult to kill and bring to shore, many narwhals are wounded by hunters and die at sea.

ICE ROUTES

Narwhals spend the winter months under the sea ice, feeding as much as they can. They surface for air at cracks and pathways, as shown here, following the same routes year after year. As climate change causes the ice to melt and shift, the patterns they have learned to follow can be disturbed. Noise pollution and shipping traffic also disrupt their natural behaviour.

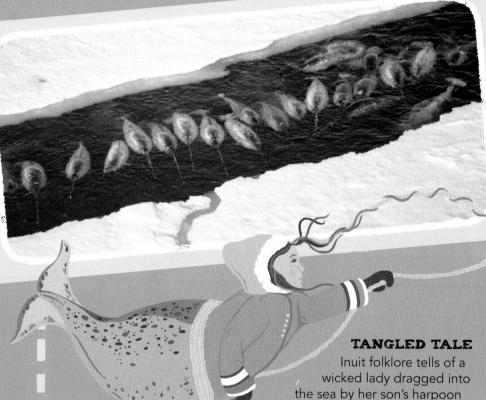

THE QUEEN'S TUSK

In the 16th century, Queen Elizabeth I received a narwhal tusk, said to be worth as much as a castle. Given as a grand gift for the wealthy, narwhal tusks were greatly admired and believed to have magical powers.

TANGLED TALE

Inuit folklore tells of a wicked lady dragged into the sea by her son's harpoon when it struck a white whale. There she became a narwhal, with her long hair creating the spiral tusk.

KEY FACTS

Scientific name: *Monodon monoceros*
Size: Length: up to 5m
Diet: Fish and squid, depending on time of year
Status: Near threatened
Amazing fact: A male's horn can be up to 3m long.

POLAR BEAR

An icon of the Arctic, the polar bear captures the human imagination. Legends describe humans copying polar bears to learn how to hunt and survive in freezing conditions. These 'sea bears' are fearsome hunters – the largest living carnivores in the world.

SEALS BEWARE

Polar bears hunt by stealth, using a clever technique known as 'still-hunting'. By locating a seal's breathing hole in the ice, a polar bear can lie in wait for its meal for several hours. Then, as soon as a seal appears, it is snatched up with lethal claws, and dragged out onto the ice. Using their strong sense of smell, polar bears will also track down seals' birthing lairs, breaking through the snow and ice with their vast bulk to catch the new seal pups inside.

FLYING BEARS

In Canada, the town of Churchill, Manitoba, is a popular place for tourists to see polar bears in the wild. For safety, any polar bears that venture too close to the town are captured by conservation officers. They are transported back to the tundra by helicopter and released in an area where they can hunt safely.

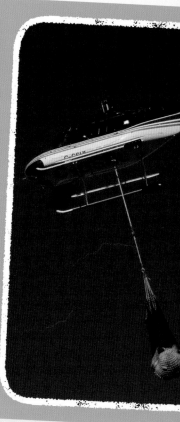

KEY FACTS

Scientific name: *Ursus maritimus*
Size: Height at shoulder: up to 1.7m; head and body length: up to 2.8m long
Diet: Mainly ringed seal pups, also bearded seals and occasionally walruses and beluga whales.

On land, polar bears feed on reindeer, seabirds, carrion and vegetation, as well as human rubbish.
Status: Vulnerable
Amazing fact: Polar bears can smell prey from up to 16km away.

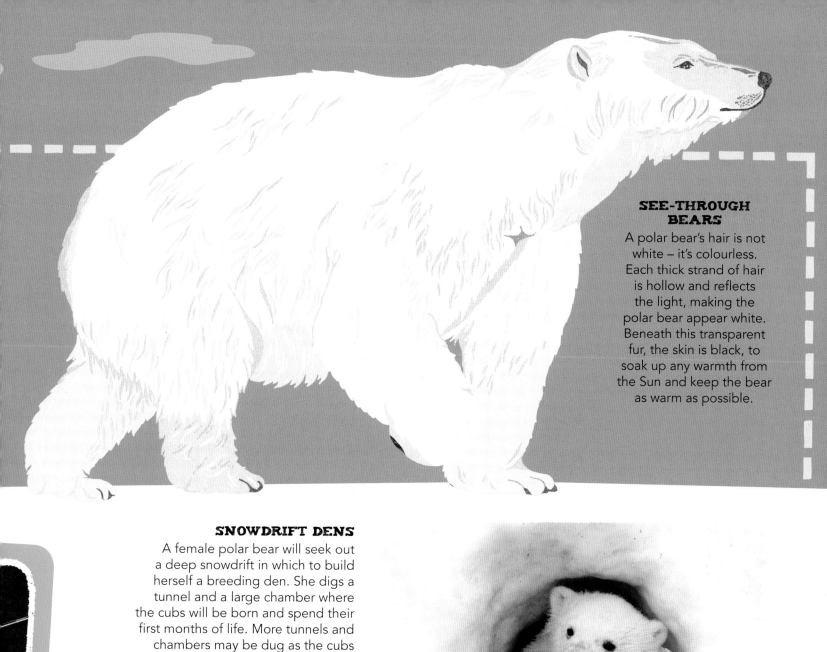

SEE-THROUGH BEARS

A polar bear's hair is not white – it's colourless. Each thick strand of hair is hollow and reflects the light, making the polar bear appear white. Beneath this transparent fur, the skin is black, to soak up any warmth from the Sun and keep the bear as warm as possible.

SNOWDRIFT DENS

A female polar bear will seek out a deep snowdrift in which to build herself a breeding den. She digs a tunnel and a large chamber where the cubs will be born and spend their first months of life. More tunnels and chambers may be dug as the cubs grow. Global warming is now affecting the snowfall, so it can be hard for polar bears to find drifts big enough for their dens.

WEATHER WARNING

The International Agreement on the Conservation of Polar Bears was signed in 1973 by every nation whose land is home to these creatures. It put an end to many years of overhunting. Polar bears are completely dependent on the Arctic ice, so their biggest threat is now climate change. With warmer waters, the sea ice melts and polar bears' hunting territories shrink. If they cannot find enough food for themselves and their cubs, polar bear numbers will continue to drop.

ARCTIC TERN

These world travellers cross the globe twice a year, avoiding the worst of the Arctic winter. With breeding grounds in the north and wintering grounds in the south, they fly between the two, making epic journeys of around 70,000km (43,496mi) each year.

Adult Arctic terns moult and replace their flight feathers over the winter.

RECORD BREAKERS

This remarkable bird has the longest migration of any animal. Trackers called geolocators are fitted to terns to record these incredible journeys. An international team of scientists has collected and studied the data. It has discovered that the sometimes strange and winding paths these birds take make the most of the wind directions. This gives them the easiest possible flight.

Arctic breeding grounds

North Atlantic food stop

Antarctic wintering ground

GONE FISHING

As they fly, Arctic terns use their sharp eyes to spot fish below. At the start of their long flight to the Antarctic, they rely on good supplies of fish in the North Atlantic, where they fill up on food while they can. In the past, the greatest risk to Arctic terns was hunting, because they were used to make fashionable hats. Today, climate change and shortage of fish are much bigger threats to the population.

Geolocators are attached to the leg of an Arctic tern to track its amazing migration.

HATCH AND HIDE

Arctic terns nest on the ground, laying eggs that look just like little rocks. When the eggs hatch, the chicks are quickly able to hide nearby, and within just three to four weeks they can fly.

KEY FACTS

Scientific name: *Sterna paradisaea*
Size: Length: up to 39cm
Diet: Small fish, crustaceans, insects
Status: Least concern (population decreasing)

Amazing fact: The long migration of this hardy seabird allows it to enjoy two summers per year and the most daylight of any creature on Earth.

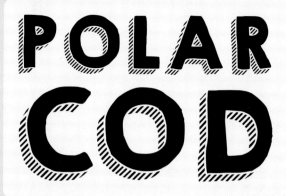

POLAR COD

Polar cod are found further north than any other fish, in the Arctic seas off Russia, Alaska, Canada and Greenland. For many Arctic creatures that feed on fish, including marine mammals, larger fish and seabirds, the polar cod are vital for survival.

ANTIFREEZE BLOOD

In temperatures where human divers need very special equipment, polar cod have everything they need on the inside. They prefer temperatures of 0–4°C (32–39°F), and can survive in even colder waters because of special 'antifreeze' proteins in their blood. These are not like the antifreeze used in cars, but they do stop ice crystals spreading through the fish's body in freezing waters.

UNDER ICE NET

Little was known about polar fish, because they live part of their lives under the mass of floating ice known as pack ice. A special net called a SUIT (Surface and Under Ice Trawl) has led to plenty of new information. This net has caught fish under the ice and its camera has taken pictures, so marine biologists can study them more closely.

PACK ICE NURSERIES

Marine research has found that billions of young polar and Arctic cod live directly below the pack ice. There they grow safely for their first years, protected from many of the sea mammals and birds that will prey on them as adults.

As global warming causes the sea ice to melt, the polar cod nurseries are threatened.

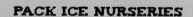

Polar cod play an important role in the food chain. They feed on plankton, then pass on energy to many other polar species when they are eaten themselves.

KEY FACTS

Scientific name: *Boreogadus saida*
Size: Length: up to 30cm
Diet: Plankton. Young polar cod eat small crustaceans called copepods; adults feed on marine worms, shrimp and adult copepods.

Status: Not evaluated
Amazing fact: Polar cod is a relative of the Atlantic cod (*Gadus morhua*), which is widely eaten by humans as fish and chips.

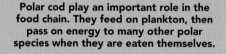

WALRUS

Bellowing, snorting herds of these marine mammals can be found lying together on Arctic ice. With a scientific name meaning 'one that walks with its teeth', the walrus is a curious creature! Its tusks grow to a metre (3ft) long and help the walrus anchor itself on the ice when it hauls its blubbery body out of the water.

HALTED HUNTING

Alaska natives hunted walruses respectfully for generations. When wider commercial hunting took over – for meat, oil and of course their impressive tusks – walruses reached the point of extinction. There are only around 200,000 walruses alive today, and only Alaska natives are allowed to hunt them. Even this permitted hunting is controlled, to make sure it is for meat and native handicrafts, with no wasteful killing of this protected species.

ORPHAN RESCUE

If walrus calves are separated from their herds they are unlikely to survive. Orphaned calves rescued by conservation officers have been hand-raised successfully.

KEY FACTS

Scientific name: *Odobenus rosmarus*
Size: Length: up to 3.5m
Diet: Bottom-dwelling invertebrates, including shellfish, worms and crustaceans. Occasionally walruses hunt seals or scavenge whale carcasses.

Status: Vulnerable
Amazing fact: Walruses look grey in the water, but on land, blood flow to the skin is increased, and walruses can appear pink.

HAULING OUT

During resting periods, and particularly during the mating season, walruses 'haul out' onto the pack ice. Global warming is causing the pack ice to melt away, causing overcrowding. Walruses are also forced to haul out onto shore instead, much further away from the rich feeding areas the young need to survive. On these overcrowded shores, the young are often trampled to death, with many hundreds killed if there is a stampede back to the water.

DEEP SEA DIVERS

Walruses can dive at speeds of 35km per hour (22mi) as deep as 500m (1,640ft), and spend as long as 40 minutes at a time under water. Down on the ocean floor, they feed in the darkness on shellfish, snails and worms.

A walrus can sleep in the water because of air sacs in its neck that act like a float, keeping its head above the surface.

NORTH & CENTRAL AMERICA

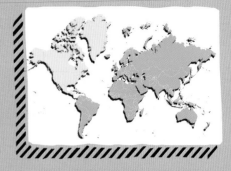

From the icy landscapes of Alaska in the north to the warm beaches of the Caribbean in the south, North and Central America offer a showcase of world habitats. Rocky mountain ranges, barren deserts, tropical swamps and lush forests form a patchwork continent that is now home to around half a billion people.

SOARING CITIES

As well as its native inhabitants, this continent has been home to people from many cultural backgrounds since explorers arrived from Europe in the 1400s. Today, some of the most heavily populated cities are found here, including New York and Mexico City, and the urban landscape continues to spread.

New York, U.S.A., and the Statue of Liberty

SIGHTS AND SCENES

This is a continent of awesome natural landmarks. It boasts Niagara Falls, the Grand Canyon and the Rocky Mountains, as well as the cloud forests of Central America and the sandy beaches of the Caribbean islands. A vast variety of wildlife depends on these very different natural environments.

Peyto Lake, Canadian Rocky Mountains

Greenland (Denmark)

Alaska (U.S.A.)

Saona Island, Dominican Republic

Canada

Hudson Bay

Pacific Ocean

United States of America

Atlantic Ocean

Mexico

Gulf of Mexico

Cuba
Jamaica
Haiti
Dominican Republic
Puerto Rico (U.S.A.)

Belize

Caribbean Sea

Guatemala
El Salvador
Honduras
Nicaragua
Costa Rica
Panama

SOUTH AMERICA

AMERICAN BEAVER

Beavers are master builders of the waterways, changing their environment to make a perfect home. Using their large front teeth, they cut down trees for food and materials to build a cosy lodge.

HOME MAKERS

Using logs, branches and mud, beavers often build lodges in ponds. If there is no pond – the beaver will create one! By building a wooden barrier called a dam, beavers make an area of still water perfect for their family home, as well as a safe place for other creatures.

Feeding chamber

Nesting chamber

Underwater entrance

Underwater entrance

A beaver lodge is a domed structure made from sticks glued together with mud. Entrances under the water lead to chambers above the waterline. The upper level of the lodge, where the beavers sleep, is kept dry and often carpeted with wood shavings.

WARNING SLAPS

Like the rudder of a boat, the beaver's flat, heavy tail helps it to move and steer through the water. A beaver will slap its tail loudly against the surface of the water, to warn its family of any danger.

BEAVER RANGERS

Humankind's relationship with the beaver has changed over the centuries. Like many creatures with soft, thick fur, beavers were hunted in large numbers during the 1800s. Hunting regulations brought this under control, so the beaver populations recovered. We now understand that beavers offer a valuable service to the waterways, acting like little wildlife rangers. Their dams help to control flooding and erosion in fast rivers, making safe places for wildlife.

KEY FACTS

Scientific name: *Castor canadensis*
Size: Head and body length: 80cm; tail length: up to 45cm
Diet: Tree bark, leaves, twigs and roots, also aquatic plants such as water lilies

Status: Least concern (population stable)
Amazing fact: As well as ordinary eyelids, beavers also have an extra see-through eyelid that acts like goggles, so they can see well under water.

GREY WOLF

A classic fairytale baddie, the grey wolf has often frightened people, but also fascinated us. Once the world's most widespread mammal, hundreds of thousands of grey wolves lived wild in North America, in harmony with the Native Americans. Since then, people have threatened these predators to the edge of extinction. Then, gradually, we have begun to help the grey wolves to recover.

WOLF FOLKLORE

In legends the wolf is linked to danger, battle and death. Wolves are often wicked characters, always planning to attack and eat up children. Some Native American tribes held a much more positive view of wolves, seeing them as protective spirits of nature, worthy of great respect. In Navajo culture, as well as many others around the world, there are stories of people shape-shifting to become werewolves.

A wolf carving on a Native American totem pole from Alaska

WOLFISH COLOURS

Around the world, the colour of a wolf's coat can vary widely. Depending on where they live, wolves can be white, cream, grey, brown and black.

Tales of wicked wolves build on people's natural fears, but in fact, wolves are more likely to avoid humans than attack them.

TWO WOLVES

A Cherokee legend tells the tale of a grandfather who told his grandson that there were two wolves fighting in him: one was evil – full of anger, greed and envy – while the other was full of kindness, peace and love. He explained that the same two wolves fight inside everybody. When the boy asked his grandfather which wolf would win, he replied, "Whichever one you feed".

KEY FACTS

Scientific name: *Canis lupus*
Size: Head and body length: 1.3m; tail length: up to 52cm
Diet: Large hooved creatures, such as moose, wild boar and wapiti (elk). Wolves hunting singly or in small groups will also eat smaller mammals.
Status: Least concern (population stable)
Amazing fact: Each wolf has its own howl – so other wolves, and scientists studying wolf packs, can use their sound to recognise individuals.

Wolves use a wide range of sounds to communicate, from soft growls and snarls to howls that travel great distances.

PACK HUNTING

In summer, wolves hunt alone, but in winter they hunt in packs, working their way across large territories, mostly at dusk and night-time. The pack travels constantly, covering sections of its territory each day seeking out enough prey to survive. To gather the pack together, or to communicate over large distances, the wolves will howl. In forests, their howls can reach wolves up to 10km (6mi) away, and in the open tundra up to 16km (10mi) away.

Wildlife biologists fit radio collars to tranquilised wolves, so they can track their location in protected areas.

WAR ON THE WOLVES

As humans took over wild areas with farmland, people began to wage war on the wolves. When farmed cattle were killed by wolves, the loss of livestock made farmers angry. They trapped and shot the wolves, earning rewards known as bounties for successful hunts.

RECONNECTING WITH THE WILD

By the 1960s, the U.S. government's efforts to destroy the wolves had almost succeeded. But these adaptable creatures were not to be destroyed – and people's feelings towards them began to change. The Endangered Animals Act of 1974 placed wolves under new protection. Steadily, wolf numbers recovered, as people became more connected with nature and interested in protecting the wildlife around them.

BALD EAGLE

As the national bird of the U.S.A., the bald eagle is a symbol of strength and freedom. It was hunted for sport, but now this bird of prey faces new threats to its wetland habitat. Fortunately, human behaviour towards this majestic bird has begun to change, just in time to save it from extinction.

The Great Seal of the United States

BACK FROM THE BRINK

Bald eagle conservation is a success story and the population is recovering. The Bald Eagle Protection Act was put in place in 1940 and continues to protect the birds and their nesting sites. Some chicks are measured and tagged, so their progress can be monitored.

GIANT NESTS

Bald eagles live near oceans, rivers or lakes, where there is plenty of aquatic life to hunt. They build some of the world's largest bird-nests, high above ground. Nesting eagles are very sensitive, and may abandon their nests or damage their eggs or young if they are startled.

DOUBLE TROUBLE

Pollution and pesticides both put the bald eagle at great risk. At the top of the food chain, bald eagles are threatened by high levels of pesticides because they fed on other animals affected by them. In 1989, when an oil tanker called the Exxon Valdez suffered a disastrous spill in Alaska, the pollution it caused killed hundreds of bald eagles.

An eagle's eyes are at least four times sharper than a human's.

Gentle enough to preen feathers and feed chicks, this beak is also sharp enough to cut flesh.

SUN DANCE

Because Native Americans believe the bald eagle is a powerful protector and messenger between the people and their gods, feathers of the high-flying bird are used in many of their ceremonies. One of the most important ceremonies is the Sun Dance, which is performed by many Plains tribes including the Blackfoot, Cheyenne and Lakota.

KEY FACTS

Scientific name: *Haliaeetus leucocephalus*
Size: Length: up to 96cm; wingspan: up to 2m
Diet: Fish, amphibians, birds, reptiles, invertebrates and small mammals
Status: Least concern (population increasing)

Amazing fact: The bald eagle isn't actually bald! Its scientific name means 'sea eagle with a white head'. The 'bald' part of their common name comes from the word 'piebald', meaning 'white-headed'.

PUMA

Also known as the cougar or mountain lion, the puma is a secretive big cat with impressive hunting skills. Its large paws pad silently across rocky ground, and it can spring from nowhere to kill its prey. This natural behaviour is sometimes misunderstood, so people develop a fear of pumas instead of understanding their true nature.

NEXT 10 MILES

NOWHERE TO HIDE

These very adaptable cats can live in a broad range of habitats, from forests and mountains to lowland and desert. Despite this, puma numbers dropped sharply when European settlers spread across their territory. Today, hunting and habitat loss continue to threaten their numbers.

Health checks and medical treatment can be given to tracked pumas.

ROAD KILL

As human settlements have spread further and further into remote areas, we have broken up puma territories and separated them from their hunting grounds. Major roads bring speeding traffic that provides another new danger for the pumas.

UNDERSTANDING THE THREAT

Pumas are shy and rarely seen by humans. They do occasionally attack – but figures show that across the U.S.A. and Canada there are only around four attacks per year. About 66,665 pumas were killed between 1907 and 1978 (according to the U.S. Fish and Wildlife Service). This is a far greater number than their threat deserves.

HOLLYWOOD

HOLLYWOOD LION

A mountain lion called P22 lives in Griffith Park, Los Angeles. Biologists from the National Park Service believe he crossed several motorways to live there, away from other males. Fitted with a tracking collar, he is carefully monitored. Photos of P22 have fascinated city-dwellers. They are a useful reminder that as humans continue to spread across the planet, we come closer to nature's other top predators.

KITTENS IN THE HILLS

Two new puma kittens, called P46 and P47, were spotted in 2015 in the Santa Monica Mountains, on the outskirts of L.A. Studies show that pumas need large territories, with connections between them. To secure the kittens' future, puma territories must be protected to allow them to mix and breed with others.

KEY FACTS

Scientific name: *Puma concolor*
Size: Length: head and body length: up to 1.5m; tail length: up to 97cm
Diet: Deer, rabbits, hares, wild pigs, porcupines

Status: Least concern (population decreasing)
Amazing fact: With a wide range that once covered most of the U.S.A., this big cat is known by more than 40 different names – the most of any mammal.

FLUTTERY DISTRACTION

Hunted by bats, which can find them in the dark with their highly tuned senses, luna moths flutter the 'tails' of their wings, distracting the hunters from their bodies. A bat may bite off the end of the wing, and the moth will still survive, protecting its furry body from a lethal attack.

LUNA MOTH

The luna moth is easy to identify, with its long, light green wings. Each of the hindwings has an 'eyespot' marking and long 'tails' or 'streamers'. New studies on the luna moth show that its wings do more than just allow it to fly...

KEEP AN EYE ON IT

The 'eyespot' markings on the luna moth's wings look like sleepy eyes, and help to put off some predators, especially birds. These markings also look like crescent moons, giving rise to the name 'luna' or 'of the Moon'.

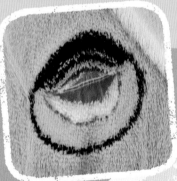

A luna moth's hindwings end with long yellow-green 'tails'.

PHEROMONE FEELERS

Female luna moths produce chemical signals called pheromones to attract males. With sensitive, feathery antennae to detect these signals, the moths can find mates over 1.6km (1mi) away.

NEW GENERATION

The female luna moth lays about 200 eggs on the underside of leaves. After about eight to 13 days, the eggs hatch and the green caterpillars begin to feed on the leaves.

LUNA LIFECYCLE

A luna moth caterpillar eats and eats, shedding its skin five times as it grows to full size. Then it spins a cocoon, in which it becomes an adult moth. When the adult first leaves its cocoon, it climbs a branch to hang its wings to dry in the air. Once the wings have filled with fluid, and night-time has come, the luna moth flies away.

LIVING DANGEROUSLY

An adult luna moth only lives for about a week. This brief time is spent avoiding attack from bats, birds, spiders and toads, as the moth tries to mate. Human settlements destroy their favourite trees, such as maple, oak and willow, while pesticides poison the leaves. Artificial light also affects the luna moth, because it finds its way using the Moon. Fluttering around a garden light uses up energy, putting its chances of finding a mate at greater risk.

KEY FACTS

Scientific name: *Actias luna*
Size: Wingspan: up to 10.5cm
Diet: Leaves (only at caterpillar stage)
Status: Not evaluated

Amazing fact: Adult luna moths do not have a mouth! At their caterpillar stage, they eat the leaves of the plant they hatched on, but as adult moths they do not feed at all.

COYOTE

The coyote has a reputation for preying on livestock and poultry, but it also plays an important role controlling rodents. These hungry predators may seem mischievous, but their hunting keeps a balance in the wildlife around them.

COYOTE OR WOLF?

COYOTE

Height: To shoulder: up to 61cm
Length: Up to 94cm
Weight: Up to 15.8kg
Ear tips: Tall and pointed
Snout shape: Narrow

GREY WOLF

Height: To shoulder: up to 81cm
Length: Up to 1.3m
Weight: Up to 62kg
Ear tips: Round
Snout shape: Broad

FRIENDS OR FOE?

Like pest controllers, coyotes reduce the numbers of any rodent that may be in plentiful supply. When humans invade their territory, or kill off their prey, coyotes simply adapt and make use of what's around them. They will feed on carrion and may also hunt livestock, making them unpopular with farmers.

MAKE DO AND MULTIPLY

Once European settlers arrived in North America, the coyote's range began to spread. Able to adapt to different habitats, coyotes benefitted from the changing landscape and the reduced numbers of wolves. Today, this resourceful animal's range includes most of Canada, the U.S.A. and Mexico.

A mythical coyote in the native style of the northwest

MISCHIEF-MAKERS

The coyote is a hero of Native American mythology. Coyotes appear in many stories as sneaky cheaters, with no rules or boundaries, or as trickster gods causing trouble. These mischief-makers often have clever survival skills and become well-loved characters.

KEY FACTS

Scientific name: *Canis latrans*
Size: Head and body: up to 94cm; tail length: up to 36cm
Diet: Almost anything! Fruit, insects, small mammals, carrion and human rubbish. Larger coyote packs can hunt larger mammals.

Status: Least concern (population increasing)
Amazing fact: Coyotes make lots of different noises, from barks and howls to yelps and squeals. They communicate with each other at dawn and dusk, and near towns they may howl at sirens.

AMERICAN BISON

The American bison has played a key role in the history of the Great Plains of the U.S.A. It was vital to the Plains Indians, and today the bison is still an important part of Plains Indian culture. Despite this, the relationship between bison and humans has been far from smooth.

WILD NO MORE

Sadly, European settlers failed to respect the bison as the Native Americans did. During the 19th century, 50 million bison were killed, for food and sport, as well as to disturb the Native American way of life. No other species on Earth has declined so quickly. Hunting laws have brought bison back from the edge of extinction, but they are considered 'ecologically extinct', because they cannot roam wild and free, other than in a few small areas.

SNAPPY BIRTHDAY

Bison calves can stand up to drink their mother's milk within 30 minutes of being born. They make a popular meal for grey wolves, grizzly bears and coyotes, so young bison are carefully guarded by their mothers.

Adult bison are the largest land mammals in North America.

SAVE THE GRASSLANDS

The grassland territory of the bison makes valuable land for farming and housing. Wild grasslands are being used up, and the wildlife that relies on them is suffering. Conservation organisations are working closely with Native American tribes to increase the bison population in protected areas. In Yellowstone National Park in the U.S.A., a herd of around 4,900 bison roam, where wild herds have lived since prehistoric times.

THE GREAT PROVIDER

In the folklore of the Great Plains tribes, the mighty bison symbolises honour, generosity and freedom. These creatures gave people not just food but also warmth from their hides and tools from their bones. A story told in many tribes called The Legend of the White Buffalo describes how the Creator will send a white bison, or a maiden dressed in white bison hide, to teach people how to pray and find peace.

CARVING THE WAY

Possibly as many as 60–90 million bison once roamed the grasslands. The herds acted like enormous lawnmowers, leaving the land just right for many smaller creatures, such as prairie dogs. In turn, the prairie dogs built underground homes that helped a host of other creatures. The bison even paved the way for people, as their seasonal migration carved paths through the wilderness.

This pipe bag is made from bison hide, which was used by Native Americans for many useful items and crafts.

NATIONAL MAMMAL OF THE U.S.A.

In 2016, the bison was chosen to be the national mammal of the U.S.A. and signed into law by President Obama. Representing America, the bison is used to symbolize strength and a connection with nature, as well as safeguarding the history of the land.

KEY FACTS

Scientific name: *Bos bison*
Size: Head and body length: up to 4m; shoulder height: up to 2m; tail length: about 40–60cm
Diet: Grasses and sedges (grass-like wetland plants)

Status: Near threatened (population stable)
Amazing fact: Bison are the heaviest land animals in North America, reaching up to 1,000kg, but despite this weight they can run at speeds of up to 65km per hour.

SOCKEYE SALMON

Waterfalls, fishermen and hungry bears are just some of the hazards these little adventurers have to overcome in their lives. At first, sockeye salmon live and feed in freshwater rivers. Most then set out for the open ocean in search of larger supplies of food, before returning to where they were born to start a new generation.

PERILS OF BEING TASTY

A popular food fish with humans and other mammals alike, the sockeye salmon forms an important part of the food chain. Hunted by larger fish as well as birds, otters, seals and sea lions, salmon help to bring nutrients from the ocean back to the creatures near the coast and inland. At spawning time, bears feast on the returning salmon as the fish make their hazardous journey upriver to spawn.

OVER-FISHING

Sockeye salmon are fished in river estuaries when they return to fresh water to breed. Worldwide, around 65 million are caught each year, not including illegal fishing. The demand for fish has become greater than the supply available. Spawning grounds are also threatened by climate change, so the future of sockeye salmon depends on carefully balanced fishing.

REACHING THE REDDS

Some groups of sockeye salmon, called kokanee, stay in fresh water. The others face the dangerous migration back from the ocean to the spawning ground, over hundreds of kilometres. Many must travel past waterfalls and rapids, leaping upstream against the current. In spawning nests, called redds, the females lay up to 5,000 orangey-red pea-sized eggs. During this time the salmon do not feed, and once they have spawned most will die.

Sockeye salmon turn a deep orangey-red from the krill they eat at sea.

LADDERS FOR FISH

Human developments along the rivers, such as dams, can be dangerous barriers to the salmons' journey. Building 'fishways' or 'fish ladders' alongside man-made structures helps the salmon reach their spawning grounds as easily as possible despite the changing landscape.

KEY FACTS

Scientific name: *Oncorhynchus nerka*
Size: Length: up to 84cm
Diet: The young feed on tiny crustaceans and insect larvae, and then plankton. Once they move out to sea, they feed on zooplankton and fish.

Status: Least concern (population stable)
Amazing fact: Depending on the depth and flow of the water, a salmon can jump several metres into the air as it battles upstream on the journey back to its spawning grounds.

CHANGING TERRITORIES

The world population of brown bears is more than 200,000. Despite this healthy number, some groups are threatened by human development. Worldwide there are 14 subspecies of brown bear. One of these, the grizzly bear, was once widespread in North America, but is now found only in western Canada and parts of western U.S.A.

BROWN BEAR

The well-known brown bear is the most widely distributed of all bears, with territories including parts of Russia, Central Asia, China, Canada and Scandinavia as well as the United States. These wide-ranging creatures now find themselves living closer to human settlements, where they are attracted to our food and waste.

IF YOU GO DOWN TO THE WOODS

Bears will feed on human rubbish, or search farms for food. Where they find food once, bears are likely to return. If humans then see them as a threat, they may be killed. Mother bears cause the most injuries and deaths to humans in North America during the summer months, often because people accidentally come between them and their cubs.

40,000 MOTHS FOR DINNER

In the mountains of Yellowstone Park, thousands of moths hide away in the rocks. The miller moth, known as the army cutworm in its caterpillar stage, is thought of by humans as a pest. To bears, it is a fatty food vital for gaining weight to survive the winter. A hungry bear can dig out around 40,000 moths each day. So far from being a pest, this moth actually keeps the bears well fed.

Brown bears use their long, curved claws for digging, fishing or killing prey.

KEY FACTS

Scientific name: *Ursus arctos*
Size: Length: up to 2.8m; tail length: up to 21cm
Diet: Plants, animals and fish. Depending where they live, bears will eat grasses, roots, nuts, berries, insects, rodents, hooved mammals and fish.
Status: Least concern (population stable)

Amazing fact: North American brown bears are not always brown – they can vary in colour from very dark brown to yellowish brown or cream. Grizzlies get their nickname, meaning 'grey haired', from their brown fur tipped with white or tan.

RUBY-THROATED HUMMINGBIRD

This little bird flashes between the flowers at great speed, drinking sugary nectar to fuel its acrobatic flights. Narrow wings help the hummingbird to fly with great precision, hovering to feed at delicate flowers, and pollinating them as it goes.

Only the males have the bright red throat that gives these birds their common name.

NON-STOP FLIGHT

Ruby-throated hummingbirds spend most of the winter in southern Mexico and Central America. In the spring, their journey back to eastern North America involves an 800km (500mi) flight over water – without stopping! They fatten up before they go, storing enough energy to allow them to cover the long distance.

SAPSUCKER WELLS

To hover, hummingbirds may beat their wings around 200 times per second.
They fly from plant to plant, visiting hundreds of flowers every day. Some woodpeckers, known as sapsuckers, leave holes in tree trunks where sap flows from the bark. These sap 'wells' and the insects that visit them make a great food source for hungry hummingbirds.

GARDEN GUEST

Human development is not always a threat to this little bird. Many people welcome these attractive garden guests with special feeders filled with sugary water. Parks, orchards and farmland also offer places to feed. Some hummingbird populations are declining, possibly because they depend on wild forest plants.

HUMMING HELICOPTERS

The clever flight skills of the hummingbird have inspired new designs for helicopter technology. Tiny micro-helicopters hover just like hummingbirds, and may be fitted with cameras to take photos of the land below.

KEY FACTS

Scientific name: *Archilochus colubris*
Size: Length: up to 9cm; wingspan: up to 11cm
Diet: Nectar
Status: Least concern (population increasing)

Amazing fact: Hummingbirds can fly upside down and backwards and hover in mid-air, but on land they struggle to walk or hop along due to their small, weak feet.

RED MEANS DANGER

An adult female black widow has a shiny black body with a red hourglass-shaped marking on the underside. She has powerful venom, so being bitten is very unpleasant, but the chance of death is actually quite small.

WESTERN BLACK WIDOW SPIDER

This little black spider is well known for its powerful venomous bite. It spins a messy, irregular web to catch its prey, and its silk is one of the strongest natural fibres in the world.

Pointed jaws with fangs

Spinnerets make silk to build webs

Four pairs of legs ending in claws

COMB FEET

Black widow spiders are part of a group known as comb-footed spiders. Stiff, jagged hairs on the 'feet' of their back legs look like combs and are used to wrap the prey in silk. Then, piercing the prey with its fangs, the spider injects special juices that turn the prey to liquid, ready to be sucked up.

DADS FOR DINNER

Here, a black widow spider hatchling crawls over its egg case. Female black widows are famous for eating the males after mating, but scientists have found that they don't usually do this. They may only kill the smaller male if he is the best prey available. Males prefer a well-fed female – partly so she can provide well for the babies – but probably also to keep themselves safe!

BULLETPROOF WEBS

The black widow spider's silk is keeping scientists very interested. Each spider makes several types of silk for different areas of its web. The 'dragline' silk that holds the spider's weight is tougher than a material called Kevlar, which is used to make bulletproof vests. The silk bends and stretches a great deal before it breaks. This natural fibre is now being copied by human technology to create special super-strong threads and ropes.

KEY FACTS

Scientific name: *Latrodectus hesperus*
Size: Length: up to 3.8cm
Diet: Flies, mosquitos, grasshoppers, beetles and caterpillars
Status: Not evaluated

Amazing fact: Black widows' venom is said to be 15 times more deadly than a rattlesnake's. Their bites are rarely fatal to adult humans, because these small spiders cannot inject very much of their powerful venom.

MONARCH BUTTERFLY

This striking, bright orange butterfly is well known for the long distance migration it makes each autumn. It travels as far as 4,800km (2,980mi) to roost over the winter in the same trees its family has used for generations. The monarch butterfly itself is not endangered globally, but its migration journey is at risk because of threats to the natural environment.

THE MAKING OF A MONARCH

After hatching from its egg, a monarch caterpillar will grow and shed its skin four times. During this time, it only feeds on the milkweed plant, which also makes the caterpillar poisonous to many of its predators. The last caterpillar stage then forms a bright green chrysalis. When it reappears as a butterfly, it is still foul-tasting and poisonous from the milkweed it fed on as a caterpillar.

FOLLOWING IN THE FOOTSTEPS

Only monarchs born late in the summer or very early in the autumn will make the long migration south, ready for the winter. These migrating butterflies never met their great-grandparents, who last made the great journey, but somehow they know exactly when and where they must go.

Canada

Rocky Mountains

Monarchs migrate south when the cold weather arrives, then return again in the spring.

Appalachian Mountains

California

U.S.A.

Some spend the winter in Mexico and others go to California, where it stays warm enough.

Mexico

KEY FACTS

Scientific name: *Danaus plexippus*
Size: Wingspan: up to 10.5cm
Diet: Caterpillars eat milkweed, adult butterflies feed on flower nectar
Status: Not evaluated but declining

Amazing fact: During migration, a monarch can travel between 80–160km per day, on a journey that can take two months to complete.

NATURE'S SPECTACLE

Gathering in millions at the same forests – sometimes even on the same trees – as their families before them, migrating monarchs are one of nature's most incredible wildlife spectacles. Now, these roosting sites are threatened with destruction as human developments spread. Butterfly reserves can limit this damage and tagging studies help to track patterns in the monarchs' behaviour.

This monarch has been tagged, so its details can be logged along its journey.

Monarch caterpillars would not survive without milkweed.

IMPORTANT POLLINATORS

Chemicals used for pest control on farmland can also kill off areas of the monarchs' milkweed. By 2015, monarch numbers had dropped by nearly a billion according to the U.S. Fish and Wildlife Service. This has another terrible effect on nature, as many plants and crops suffer without monarchs to pollinate them. Schools and nature organisations now encourage people to plant milkweed to help these important pollinators.

RED-EYED TREE FROG

This shockingly bright little night-hunter can hide away during the day, despite its bright colours, making itself barely visible against the rainforest leaves. On full display, hopping from branch to branch, the red-eyed tree frog is easily recognised, and has become a popular symbol in the fight to save its threatened rainforest home.

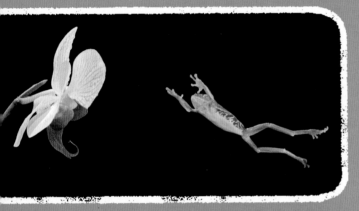

STICKY FINGERS

The red-eyed tree frog is arboreal – meaning it lives in the trees. Suction cups on its feet allow it to grip the leaves as it jumps and climbs through the forest. To catch prey, it shoots out its long, sticky tongue.

Powerful legs and suction cups on its feet make the red-eyed tree frog an excellent climber.

STARTLE COLOURATION

Hiding away underneath leaves in the day, this frog cleverly covers its blue and yellow flashes and orange feet, shutting its eyes to make it appear completely green. If a predator comes along, the frog will flash its large red eyes and reveal its brightly coloured sides, hoping to shock the enemy just long enough for an escape.

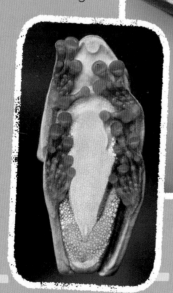

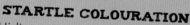

A red-eyed tree frog's vivid colours can be hidden away or used to shock.

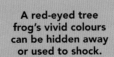

ONE TO WATCH

The red-eyed tree frog is not currently endangered, but frogs react very quickly to changes in their environment. They are known as 'indicator species', because if their numbers drop it can warn us about damage to the environment. Use of pesticides and fertilisers as well as climate change and acid rain can all affect these frogs, as well as their eggs and tadpoles.

KEY FACTS

Scientific name: *Agalychnis callidryas*
Size: Length: up to 8cm
Diet: The tadpoles filter feed, the adults eat insects
Status: Least concern

Amazing fact: A female red-eyed tree frog may carry a male on her back for several hours while she chooses where to lay eggs. Only then can he fertilise them.

WESTERN DIAMOND-BACKED RATTLESNAKE

Its diamond markings and rattling sound make this snake an iconic creature of the southwest of the United States. The shivering rattle often announces the western diamond-backed rattlesnake before it is seen, giving a clear warning to back off to avoid a venomous attack.

BEWARE Rattlesnakes!

HEAT HUNTERS

Western diamond-backed rattlesnakes eat about once every two to three weeks and can sometimes go for up to two years without food. They lie in wait around burrows, using sight, smell and heat-sensitive pits between their eyes and nostrils to pinpoint their prey. Once a creature is killed and swallowed, the snake's venom continues to break it down so it can be digested.

HEAR THE WARNING

Each year, around 7–8,000 people are bitten by snakes in the U.S.A. Luckily, there is now very little risk that these bites will be deadly – only an estimated one in 50 million people will be killed by a snakebite. Despite this small risk, most of the deadly bites are made by the eastern and western diamond-backed rattlesnakes, so the warning sound of the rattle is certainly not to be ignored.

Venom is collected or 'milked' for research and to create the antivenom treatment for snakebites.

The rattle is made of segments that knock together when the tail is shaken.

BABY'S NEW RATTLE

These rattlesnakes do not lay eggs like many other snakes, but give birth to as many as 60 live babies. Newborn rattlesnakes are born with fangs and toxic venom, but their rattles are grown in segments each time they moult their skin.

KEY FACTS

Scientific name: *Crotalus atrox*
Size: Length: up to 2.3m
Diet: Small mammals and birds
Status: Least concern (population stable)

Amazing fact: Rattlesnakes' rattles are made up of a protein called keratin – the same protein that makes human hair and fingernails.

SOUTH AMERICA

South America boasts such a variety of climates that a tour of the continent will include tropical rainforests, vast dry deserts and the snow-capped mountains of the Andes. The Atlantic Ocean lies to the east and the Pacific to the west, while one of the world's longest rivers, the Amazon, snakes its way across the continent. The Amazon rainforest, the world's largest tropical forest, makes South America home to millions of different species of animals and plants.

Carribean Sea

Venezuela

Colombia

Galápagos Islands (Ecuador)

Ecuador

Guyana Suriname

French Guiana

North Atlantic Ocean

Peru

Brazil

Bolivia

South Pacific Ocean

Paraguay

Uruguay

Argentina

South Atlantic Ocean

Chile

LAND OF WONDER

Natural wonders include the world's highest waterfall, Angel Falls in Venezuela, and the vast plains of the Atacama desert in Chile. In Peru sits Machu Picchu – a breathtaking city built more than 500 years ago during the Inca Empire.

CITY SIGHTS

Brazil has some of the biggest cities in the world. More than 15 million people live in São Paulo, while in Rio de Janeiro the statue of Christ the Redeemer overlooks the vast city from Mount Corcovado.

CARNIVAL CULTURE

South America is home to around 390 million people. As well as the indigenous people, who include the Arawaks, Kalina and Guarani, many others have settled here from Europe, Africa and Japan. Each year, Brazil is host to the biggest carnival in the world – a cultural celebration that fills the streets of Rio with spectacular costumes and parades.

TROOP TACTICS

Adult male howler monkeys are dark reddish-brown with some golden fur on their backs, while the females and babies are often lighter. A group of howlers, called a troop, needs several hectares of forest to form its territory.

GUIANAN RED HOWLER MONKEY

While many animals hide, this noisy monkey makes itself known at an incredible volume. Travelling from tree to tree in the rainforests of northern South America, Guianan red howler monkeys fiercely defend their territory with their calls.

HOWLING TROOPS

At dawn and dusk, a troop of howler monkeys will call, sending a clear message to others as far as 5km (3mi) away that the territory is taken. In males, a bone in the throat called the hyoid bone is enlarged, making their calls louder. Once the leading males begin howling, other members of the troop join in.

FOREST THREATS

The destruction of the rainforest threatens howler monkeys, and they are also at risk from hunters who sell them as 'bushmeat'. Their diet of fruits and vegetation means that they spread seeds everywhere they go. Any threat to the howler monkey population soon becomes a risk to the forest itself, because new growth relies on their seed-filled dung.

GOD OF THE ARTS

For the Mayan people, a howler monkey was the god of art and music. At a temple in the Mayan city of Copan, large statues shaking rattles are believed to be howler monkey gods.

KEY FACTS

Scientific name: *Alouatta macconnelli*
Size: Head and body length: up to 63cm; tail length: up to 80cm
Diet: Fruit, flowers, leaves, tree bark and moss
Status: Least concern

Amazing fact: Howler monkeys are the loudest land animals in the world. Of living creatures, only the blue whale can beat them on volume.

NINE-BANDED ARMADILLO

The name 'armadillo' means 'little armoured one' in Spanish and it is the only living mammal with a tough, flexible shell called a carapace. The nine-banded armadillo, also known as the long-nosed armadillo, is a secretive but surprising creature that has proved itself to be a medical marvel.

SHOCK FACTOR

Armadillos are at risk from many natural predators, including cougars, coyotes, maned wolves and bears. When startled, an armadillo may jump about a metre (3ft) in the air to confuse a predator. Unfortunately, this technique does not help them with the danger of traffic. Road collisions kill thousands of armadillos every year, making humans their greatest threat.

MUSICAL SHELLS

The armadillo's shell is made up of about 2,000 scales called scutes. Together, these make two protective shields, joined in the middle by eight or nine softer bands, which give this species its name. Traditionally, the Quechua and Aymara people used the shells to make an instrument called a charango, which is now made from wood.

MEDICAL MARVELS

This particular armadillo helps medical scientists in some very unusual ways. Nine-banded armadillos have played a key role in helping scientists understand a dangerous disease called leprosy (or Hansen's disease), leading to treatments that have saved millions of people. They have also helped doctors learn more about multiple births, because they always give birth to four identical babies.

KEY FACTS

Scientific name: *Dasypus novemcinctus*
Size: Length: up to 80cm including tail
Diet: Beetles and other invertebrates (also occasionally small amphibians and reptiles, young mammals and birds' eggs)
Status: Least concern (population stable)

Amazing fact: There are many species of armadillo, ranging in size from the pink fairy armadillo (*Chlamyphorus truncates*) at just up to 15cm long including its tail, to the giant armadillo (*Priodontes maximus*), which is up to 1.5m long including its tail.

LLAMA

Llamas were domesticated from the wild guanaco, and there are now around four million of these popular farm animals in South America, with many more worldwide. Their ancestors migrated from North America around 2.5 million years ago.

GUARD LLAMAS

Some young llamas will bond quickly with sheep or goats, and will defend them against predators. They make good guards, keeping watch over a herd and making a loud alarm call if they spot any threat.

LLAMA JERKY

The Incas, and the Quechuas after them, enjoyed dried llama meat called 'Ch'arki'. It was dried under the Sun and salted to make a delicious and long-lasting product. Later, American cowboys liked the Ch'arki and began to make their own dried meat from beef, calling it 'jerky'.

FARMERS' FRIENDS

Relatives of the camel, but without a hump, llamas and alpacas make reliable work animals. These bright, friendly creatures earned their place as popular pack animals, offering lots of useful services to their owners. Inca people used them for transport as well as farming them for meat, wool and leather.

PRECIOUS POO

Llama dung was very valuable both as a fertilizer and as fuel to native South American people. It helped crops grow successfully even in poor soil, giving Inca societies extra food that they could sell. Descendants of the Inca peoples, such as the Quechuas and Aymaras, still farm llamas today.

KEY FACTS

Latin name: *Lama glama*
Size: Length: up to 1.2m; height to shoulder: about 1.2m
Diet: Shrubs, lichens, vegetation
Status: Domestic animal, not at risk

Amazing fact: Llamas may be hardworking creatures, but if they are overloaded they will refuse to move, and may hiss or spit in protest.

GREEN ANACONDA

This giant snake can weigh up to 227 kilograms (550 lbs) and open its jaws wide enough to swallow even large prey whole. The anaconda is the heaviest snake, and the thickness of its body makes it a particularly strong and deadly predator.

SUPERSIZE MEALS

A green anaconda's diet includes fish, turtles and birds, as well as mammals ranging from rodents to marsh deer. Large adult green anacondas can even kill caiman, as shown below, though not without a fierce fight. Using the power of its body, the green anaconda grabs prey and coils tightly around it, eventually killing it. If it is near water, it may drown its prey.

NO PREDATORS

While young anacondas are at risk from predators, adults have little to fear except for humans. These large reptiles are hunted, both legally and illegally, for their richly patterned, glossy skin to be sold as leather goods. Young anacondas are also captured for the illegal pet trade.

Stretchy ligaments in its jaw allow the anaconda to swallow prey whole.

KEY FACTS

Scientific name: *Eunectes murinus*
Size: Length: up to 9.6m
Diet: Fish, other reptiles, birds and mammals
Status: Not evaluated

Amazing fact: The green anaconda is the largest species of snake on Earth today. Fossil discoveries show that prehistoric species, such as the giant *Titanoboa*, grew even larger.

SAVE THE SNAKES

In some countries where the green anaconda lives, there are laws to control hunting and make snakeskin goods illegal. Despite this, people's fear of the anaconda often leads to the snakes being harmed.

One of the biggest challenges in protecting both the snakes and the local people is keeping an accurate record of anaconda numbers in the deep, dark waters of the rainforest.

BREEDING BALL

Male green anacondas are smaller than the females. At breeding time many males will gather to mate with a single female, forming a wriggly mass called a 'breeding ball'. The female will mate with several males, and she may eat some of them too!

GOLIATH BIRD-EATING SPIDER

This enormous hairy spider can grow to the size of a dinner plate. Its fearsome name comes from the descriptions given by Victorian explorers, who saw this species eating a hummingbird. In fact, it rarely finds birds during its night-time hunt, and tends to feed on creatures it catches near its burrow.

Venom is injected through long fangs.

Two pedipalps help the spider hold its prey ready to bite.

FANGTASTIC

The Goliath bird-eating spider is part of the group of spiders called tarantulas. It has a venomous bite and long fangs, but will only use them on humans if it is threatened. The bite, described as feeling like a wasp sting, may be painful but it is unlikely to kill.

TRAPPED AND TRANSPORTED

The territory of this large spider is being reduced as the rainforest is destroyed. They have also become very popular as pets and exhibits in zoos. These spiders are captured in the wild and transported to sell, but many die on the journeys. There are very few laws in place to control the collection of these spiders from the wild. Captive breeding programmes are now under way, so that this impressive hunter can be studied more closely and given better protection.

SPIDER'S SURPRISE

As well as venom, the Goliath bird-eating spider has another surprise for attackers. By rubbing its body with its legs, it can release tiny barbed hairs known as urticating hairs. These are very irritating to humans and can cause painful rashes.

ROASTED SPIDER

In north-eastern South America, native people still catch and eat Goliath bird-eating spiders, serving them roasted in banana leaves. The irritating hairs have to be removed first and the cooked meat is said to taste like shrimp.

KEY FACTS

Scientific name: *Theraphosa blondi*
Size: Leg span: up to 30cm
Diet: Insects, frogs, small snakes, lizards, rodents and bats. The spider's name comes from the fact that it can, very occasionally, feed on small birds.

Status: Not evaluated
Amazing fact: The Goliath bird-eating spider's leg span is second in width to the giant huntsman spider, but its much bulkier body makes it the largest spider in the world by mass.

MANED WOLF

Is it a wolf, or a fox, or a dog? Or is it perhaps a coyote or a jackal? Actually, the maned wolf is none of these, but it does belong to the same family, Canidae. It has long legs that allow it to see over the long grass, and a dark mane of fur that spikes upwards if it is threatened, making it appear bigger and more fierce.

WOLF APPLES

One of the maned wolf's favourite foods is the lobeira fruit, known as the 'wolf apple'. The wolf spreads the fruit's seeds across its territory in its dung. Leaf cutter ants collect the dung to use on fungus gardens in their nests. Then, they carry the unwanted fruit seeds to waste patches where more lobeira plants then grow. In this way, the maned wolf and the ants provide each other with very helpful gardening services.

SAVING THE CERRADO

Maned wolves were hunted by native South Americans, especially for their eyes, which are thought to bring good luck. They have also been targeted by farmers, particularly if they feed on poultry. Laws now protect them in parts of South America. Today, maned wolves are at risk from damage to their habitat, known as the 'cerrado'. As human developments spread into this wooded grassland area, traffic kills many maned wolves and their cubs.

Sometimes known as the 'fox on stilts', the maned wolf has particularly long legs.

KEY FACTS

Scientific name: *Chrysocyon brachyurus*
Size: Head and body length: up to 1.1m; tail length: up to 50cm
Diet: Mostly fruits and vegetation, as well as small mammals, reptiles, insects and birds
Status: Near threatened (population trend unknown)

Amazing fact: The smell of a maned wolf's urine (wee) is so strong that in captivity visitors can smell them before they see them. Using this stinky spray to mark its territory has earned this creature the nickname 'skunk wolf'.

TOCO TOUCAN

Famous for its large, brightly coloured beak, the toco toucan is an icon of the South American rainforests. As well as being a good feeding tool, the beak has other uses that scientists are still investigating. Easily recognised, the toco toucan has appeared on stamps, adverts and campaigns to save the rainforests.

In relation to its body size, the toco toucan has the largest beak of all birds.

BUSY BEAKS

Scientists believe the toco toucan's huge beak has several purposes. It is certainly useful for feeding, allowing the toucan to pick and peel fruit easily. It may also help the toucan to attract a mate, or act as a bright warning to scare away rivals. A toucan can also control its temperature using its large beak – allowing more blood to flow to the beak if it needs to cool down.

SEEN AND HEARD

Toco toucans adapt well to new habitats and are not currently endangered. They live in small flocks and communicate with a croaky call. Their sounds and colours can put the toucan at risk from hunters, and young birds may be captured for the pet trade.

Stretching from a low branch, this toucan takes a drink.

FRUIT TOSS

Watching them in the wild, scientists have noticed that pairs of toucans will toss fruit to each other, as a mating ritual. Recording this behaviour and studying breeding patterns helps scientists to understand more about these birds. This knowledge will help us to conserve the rainforest habitat of the toco toucans, before they are at risk at all.

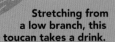

KEY FACTS

Scientific name: *Ramphastos toco*
Size: Length: up to 63cm; wingspan: similar to body length
Diet: Mainly fruit; sometimes young birds, eggs, lizards and insects

Status: Least concern (population decreasing)
Amazing fact: Its beak may be large but the toco toucan's wings are small. It doesn't need to fly far as it lives where there are plenty of trees.

BAT ATTACK

As well as flying with its leathery wings, a vampire bat can crawl, walk and leap onto the legs and bodies of the animals it will feed on. Biting a little flap in the skin with its small but sharp front teeth, the vampire bat laps up the blood.

COMMON VAMPIRE BAT

This flying mammal is well known for feeding on blood. It tends to feed in the dark on sleeping animals, so it is often feared and misunderstood. Vampire stories and movies dramatise its behaviour, so this specialised feeder is mistakenly thought to be a blood-thirsty killer.

LITTLE DRACULAS

Vampire bats have special saliva that stops blood from clotting. This has been used to make a new human medicine nicknamed 'draculin', after the famous fictional vampire Count Dracula. By helping to break down blood clots, this can save the lives of people with heart conditions.

CONTROL AND CAUTION

Vampire bats can be carriers of diseases including rabies. Colonies of vampire bats are sometimes destroyed to try to prevent the disease spreading. In some cases, the wrong species is targeted, killing off other bats that are very useful in controlling insect populations or spreading the seeds of fruit trees.

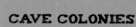

CAVE COLONIES

These successful night-hunters live in groups of 30–150, in caves, hollow trees, old buildings and mines. They can be considered a pest where they feed on the blood of livestock. Vampire bats can also feed on human blood, though this is rare.

KEY FACTS

Scientific name: *Desmodus rotundus*
Size: Head and body length: up to 9cm
Diet: Blood
Status: Least concern (population stable)

Amazing fact: A vampire bat's teeth are so sharp that its bite may not be felt at all. Their saliva dulls any pain, so a bat may drink its victim's blood for up to 30 minutes.

JAGUAR

At the top of the food chain, known as an apex predator, the jaguar's name means 'he who kills with one leap'. With a muscular body and sharp teeth, this big cat can overpower prey as large as deer, cattle and caimans. Their beautiful coat patterns put them at high risk from hunters, and as their forest territory continues to shrink, these wild cats need human protection.

PAW PRINT FUR

To tell the difference between a jaguar and a leopard, the clue is in the spots. Unlike the leopard, the jaguar has spots inside its rosette-shaped circular markings. South American folklore says these were caused by the jaguar dabbing mud on with its paws, for better camouflage in the shadows. Big cats with mostly black fur are commonly known as black panthers.

Jaguar fur

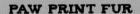

Leopard fur

JAGUAR GODS

These powerful big cats captured the imaginations of many South and Central American peoples. Mayans used jaguars to symbolise the 'night sun' of the underworld, and native peoples of the Amazon believed the Sun itself created these big cats. Many peoples worshipped jaguar gods, featuring them in their artwork and monuments.

This Inca ornament is a jaguar made of embossed gold.

This jaguar cub is being weighed. Orphaned cubs must be carefully monitored and taught how to live in the wild.

UMBRELLA SPECIES

In Central and South America, there are thought to be around 15,000 jaguars in the wild, but their habitat is shrinking as the land is changed into farmland. Jaguars help to control the numbers of small grazing animals, that would otherwise strip the land of vegetation. They are known as an 'umbrella species', because protecting jaguars and their needs will, in turn, protect other wildlife in their habitat.

KEY FACTS

Scientific name: *Panthera onca*
Size: Head and body length: up to 1.7m; tail length: 40–80cm
Diet: Jaguars are carnivores. Prey includes various mammals and reptiles, depending on location.

Status: Near threatened (population decreasing)
Amazing fact: The jaguar is the third largest cat in the world, and the biggest in the Americas. It can see in the dark six times better than a human.

CATTLE

From large, wild ancestors called aurochs, today we have around 1.4 billion domestic cattle in the world, with hundreds of breeds. Brazil in South America exports the most beef around the world, making billions of dollars a year. Cattle products are so popular it is difficult to imagine life without them.

STRONG ROOTS

In the 1900s, cattle called zebu were brought to Brazil and bred with European cattle. Zebu have humps on their shoulders and a fold of skin under the neck. They originated in Southern Asia and are well adapted to the heat of the tropics. This gave farmers good beef and dairy breeds that were also hardy enough to thrive in South America.

MILK AND MONEY

The Food and Agriculture Organisation recorded that there were 271 million dairy cows in the world in 2013. The Holstein-Friesian breed is the largest milk producer, with each cow capable of making more than 20 litres (35 pints) of milk per day.

The markings on the hides of Holstein-Friesian cows are like fingerprints – no two individuals have exactly the same pattern.

THE SACRED COW

In the Hindu religion cows are sacred – they symbolise life and the Earth, playing an important part in festivals celebrating nature. In most of the states of India it is illegal to eat beef (cattle meat). Cows are seen as important providers, giving milk and other dairy products. Their dung makes a valuable fertiliser, or can be used as fuel.

A cow and calf of the very popular Hereford breed

BEEFY PROFITS

Cattle were highly valued by early cultures because they provided milk, meat and leather. Today these products have become global industries. There are more than 210 million cattle in Brazil, and the demand for grazing land now threatens the rainforest – home to many endangered creatures.

KEY FACTS

Family: *Bos taurus*
Size: Length: 1.2–1.5m; height to shoulder: 1.2–1.4m
Diet: Pasture (grasses and hay) and cattle feeds made from grains

Status: Domestic animal, not evaluated
Amazing fact: Cattle are ruminant mammals. This means that after swallowing food, they bring it back up to chew again, sometimes several times.

MANED THREE-TOED SLOTH

The sleepy nature of this furry sloth captures the human imagination as it snoozes in the trees. Looking beyond their relaxed lifestyle, scientists have discovered the sloth has a remarkable ability to recover quickly from injury. There are four different species of three-toed sloth today – all now facing serious threats to their forest homes.

LIFE IN THE SLOW LANE

Hiding in the trees, like a bundle of dried leaves, the sloth lives a slow life. It comes down only to empty its bowels (poo) or to move to another tree that is out of reach. On the ground, it cannot stand or walk, but drags itself along using its claws. A sloth's rough, algae-covered fur is home to ticks, mites, and as many as 120 *Cryptoses* moths, which lay their eggs in sloth dung.

BROKEN HOMELAND

Maned three-toed sloths live in areas of rainforest along the Atlantic coast of Brazil, where many are injured by human activity. There are now rescue centres where injured or orphaned sloths are treated and cared for.

SUPERHERO SKILLS

Sloths may be slow on land and sleepy in the trees, but they can swim well. Surprisingly, they also heal very quickly, even from bad injuries. Further study may show if this survival skill could benefit human medicine. Only if the sloth population is protected will we discover more about this very useful ability.

Pygmy three-toed sloth swimming

CORRIDORS TO SAFETY

As more and more of the rainforest is cleared, the maned three-toed sloth's future is very uncertain. To survive, they need protected corridors of forest to join up their separate areas. Without these, the slow sloths will have little hope of mixing to breed with others.

KEY FACTS

Scientific name: *Bradypus torquatus*
Size: Head and body length: up to 70cm; tail length: up to 9cm
Diet: Mostly young leaves, with occasional twigs and buds

Status: Vulnerable (population decreasing)
Amazing fact: A sloth's fur can appear greenish due to algae. This helps the sloth to stay hidden, and makes up part of its diet.

TERMITE

Towering termite mounds are one of nature's most incredible homes. Some wood-eating termites can cause terrible damage to human structures, but out in the dry lands of South America the mound-building termites play a useful role. These termites and their carefully constructed homes provide food and shelter for many other species.

INCREDIBLE ARCHITECTS

Working in their millions, these tiny creatures can create amazing structures. Workers build the cone-shaped nest, which is protected by a hard wall. Inside the mound is a network of small chambers and an oval-shaped 'hive' in the middle. Workers also bring food, while soldiers defend the nest with their enlarged jaws.

MIGHTY MOUNDS

Termites' tunnels help the soil to absorb rainwater more easily, and the plant matter that these insects bring to the nest acts as fertiliser for the surrounding area. These moist, fertile areas are perfect for plant life to grow, which then attracts grazing creatures.

DAZZLING DOMES

The Emas National Park in Brazil is a World Heritage Site, meaning it has outstanding importance to world wildlife and culture. Here, at night, it is sometimes possible to find termite mounds lit up like Christmas trees. This is due to a creature known as the headlight beetle, which lays its eggs in the walls of termite mounds. When the beetle larvae hatch, their bodies glow like bright green lights to attract flying ants and termites to eat.

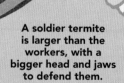

A soldier termite is larger than the workers, with a bigger head and jaws to defend them.

KEY FACTS

Scientific name: *Cornitermes cumulans*
Size: Body length: around 6mm
Diet: Dead wood, grass, fallen leaves
Status: Not evaluated

Amazing fact: Termites build the largest and most complex nests of all insects. Some may reach over 1m in height and width at the base.

GALÁPAGOS TORTOISE

On the Galápagos Islands near Ecuador in South America, populations of giant tortoise fascinate scientists and tourists alike. Some of these giants can weigh up to 250 kilograms (550 lbs) – roughly the same as a brown bear! When numbers dropped to near extinction in the 1970s, an urgent and challenging conservation effort began.

DARWIN AND THE BEAGLE

On his voyage aboard the *Beagle* in 1835, naturalist Charles Darwin spotted that the sizes and shapes of these tortoises varied with each island he visited. This eventually helped Darwin form his Theory of Evolution, which made him one of the most important scientists in history. One of the groups of tortoises, *Chelonoidis nigra darwini*, was named after him.

PIRATE FOOD

Sailors, including pirates and explorers, brought tortoises on board as a source of fresh, tasty meat. Not only were they easy to catch, but they could also live a year or more without food or water.

KEY FACTS

Scientific name: *Chelonoidis nigra porteri*
Size: Carapace length: up to 1.5m
Diet: Cacti, grass, nettles, lichens and fruit
Status: Endangered

Amazing fact: Galápagos tortoises can live to well over 100 years old. One called Harriet lived to about 169 years old.

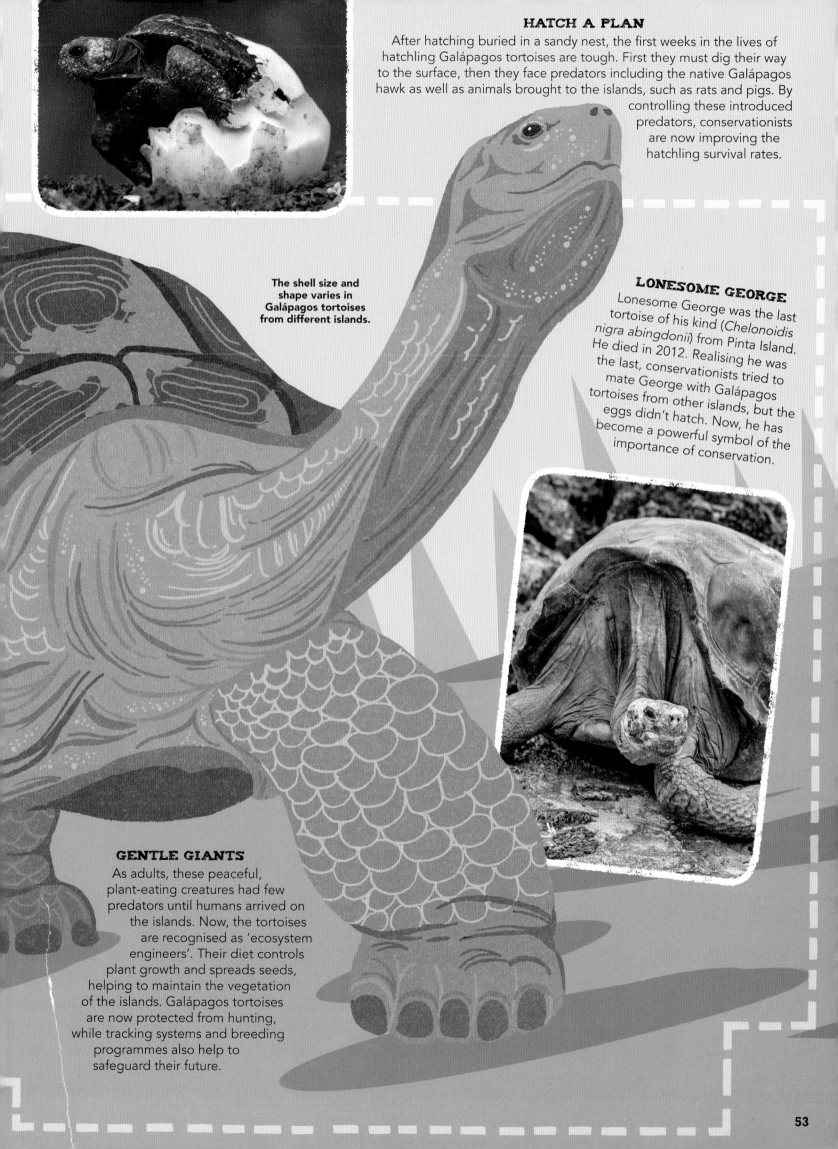

HATCH A PLAN

After hatching buried in a sandy nest, the first weeks in the lives of hatchling Galápagos tortoises are tough. First they must dig their way to the surface, then they face predators including the native Galápagos hawk as well as animals brought to the islands, such as rats and pigs. By controlling these introduced predators, conservationists are now improving the hatchling survival rates.

The shell size and shape varies in Galápagos tortoises from different islands.

LONESOME GEORGE

Lonesome George was the last tortoise of his kind (*Chelonoidis nigra abingdonii*) from Pinta Island. He died in 2012. Realising he was the last, conservationists tried to mate George with Galápagos tortoises from other islands, but the eggs didn't hatch. Now, he has become a powerful symbol of the importance of conservation.

GENTLE GIANTS

As adults, these peaceful, plant-eating creatures had few predators until humans arrived on the islands. Now, the tortoises are recognised as 'ecosystem engineers'. Their diet controls plant growth and spreads seeds, helping to maintain the vegetation of the islands. Galápagos tortoises are now protected from hunting, while tracking systems and breeding programmes also help to safeguard their future.

HORSE

Horses and humans have had a special relationship for thousands of years. Used for work, transport and leisure, there are now more than 300 breeds of horse in the world and many industries dependent on them.

HARDY HORSES

The South American Criollo breed has a strong, muscly body, making it well suited to hard work. Their ancestors came from Spain, brought by European explorers. Later, gauchos (cowboys) took wild Criollos from the pampas grasslands, putting their strength and stamina to good work with herds of cattle.

THE BEST OF FRIENDS

Humans have relied on the help of horses for thousands of years. Today, we use domesticated horses for leisure, farming, transport and even for police and army work. No other creature has offered so many opportunities to humankind. Sports that involve horses – known as equestrian events – are hugely popular, including racing, dressage, gymkhana and polo. Polo ponies are often bred from Criollo horses and thoroughbreds, to give them stamina and speed.

EASY RIDER

The Peruvian Paso horse is a breed well loved for its smooth ride and unique gait that can cover long distances comfortably. Horses are an important part of the cultural heritage of Peru, where annual competitions and festivals are held to celebrate the Peruvian Paso.

KEY FACTS

Scientific name: *Equus caballus*
Size: Height to shoulder: up to 2m (Criollo breed: up to 1.5m)
Diet: Grasses and other leafy flowering plants
Status: Domestic animal, not evaluated

Amazing fact: It is estimated there are more than 58 million horses in the world, but only one species remains in the wild – the endangered Przewalski's horse.

HYACINTH MACAW

With striking royal blue feathers and flashes of bright yellow skin around the eyes, hyacinth macaws are beautiful birds that inspire people to visit them in their natural environment. The largest parrot in the world, this playful bird suffers mainly from the illegal pet trade but also from the destruction of its habitat.

NUTTY NIBBLER

A strong beak and boned tongue help the hyacinth macaw with its diet of hard palm nuts. One of these – the acuri nut – has a shell so hard that macaws prefer to eat them when they have passed through the guts of cattle and come out softened in the dung.

PICKY PARROTS

The Brazilian tropical wetland region known as the Pantanal is home to the largest population of hyacinth macaws. They choose nesting sites carefully, preferring soft-wooded maduvi trees that are at least 60 years old. Cutting down maduvi trees has a long-term damaging effect on breeding.

BLUES ON THE BRINK

There are thought to be around 6,500 hyacinth macaws in the wild. Other Brazilian blue macaws are even closer to extinction. Despite laws to protect them, around 10,000 hyacinth macaws were caught during the 1980s to be sold in the pet trade. Young hyacinth macaws are still taken from the wild by smugglers who try to sell them for thousands of dollars.

PARROT PROTECTION

Conservation efforts with hyacinth macaws have been very successful. As part of the Hyancinth Macaw Project in the Pantanal's Caiman Ecological Refuge, nesting behaviour has been studied and artificial nests have been built in the right trees with great care. These extra nests, along with tracking systems, have greatly improved macaw numbers.

KEY FACTS

Scientific name: *Anodorhynchus hyacinthus*
Size: Length including tail: up to 1m
Diet: Palm nuts, and occasionally seeds and snails

Status: Vulnerable (population decreasing)
Amazing fact: In the wild, hyacinth macaws can live to 60 years old, and even longer in captivity.

EUROPE

The second smallest continent, but the third most populated by people, Europe spans more than 40 countries. Many of these enjoy a mild climate, but there are extremes of cold in the north, while in the south the Mediterranean is dry and warm. Europe is home to a broad range of animal species, many living very close to human settlements. On this crowded continent, areas of natural wilderness are limited.

ALPINE VIEWS

The Alps are a mountain system, just north of the Mediterranean Sea, stretching around 1,200km (750mi). The highest point is Mont Blanc at over 4,800m (15,748ft). To the east, Europe is separated from Asia by another mountain range, the Urals.

PEOPLE POWER

The population of Europe is estimated to be around 739 million. This means that about 10 per cent of the world's entire population lives here. Europe is home to many nature conservation organisations working to protect wildlife globally.

Paris, France

LIVING HISTORY

Early civilisations in Europe, such as the ancient Greeks and Romans, had a powerful effect on the landscape. As societies thrived, towns and cities grew and the urban environment spread across the continent.

The Parthenon, Greece

Barents Sea

Iceland

Norwegian Sea

Sweden

Finland

Norway

Estonia

Russia

Latvia

Scotland

Denmark
Netherlands
Luxembourg
Belgium

Russia Lithuania

Northern Ireland
Ireland
Wales
England

Belarus

Germany

Poland

North Atlantic Ocean

France

Czech Republic

Slovakia

Ukraine

Austria

Hungary

Italy

Romania

Serbia

Moldova

Bulgaria

Greece

Black Sea

Portugal

Spain

Slovenia
Croatia

Switzerland

Caspian Sea

Malta

Macedonia

Bosnia & Herzegovina

Kosovo
Albania
Montenegro

Cyprus

Mediterranean Sea

ASIA

AFRICA

TAWNY OWL

As the most common and widespread owl in Europe, the tawny owl's hooting call is a well-known night-time sound. With its range spreading into North Africa and Asia, the tawny owl is not endangered, but it suffers from living near to human activity.

TAWNY TERRITORY

Tawny owls pair for life and stay in their nesting territory all year. Nests are made in tree hollows, or in other abandoned nests. The female lays two to five white eggs, each about a week apart, so the young hatch at different times. When they leave the nest, they each form a territory of their own.

FLYING THE NEST

Young owlets sometimes leave their nests before they are fully able to fly. They hide away at first on branches or on the ground, but they are surprisingly skilled at climbing back to the nest. Unless an owlet is discovered injured or in danger, it should be left alone to climb back to safety.

NEST AWARENESS

Human disturbance often puts tawny owls and their young at risk. When trees are cut down this leads to a lack of nesting sites. In some areas of protected woodland, as well as parks and large gardens, nest boxes can be a helpful way of providing a safe home for tawny owls.

KEY FACTS

Scientific name: *Strix aluco*
Size: Length: up to 39cm; wingspan: up to 1.4m
Diet: Small rodents, voles, frogs and beetles
Status: Least concern (population stable)

Amazing fact: The familiar 'twit-twoo' sound of the tawny owl comes from a male and female pair. The female's main call is the 'twit' or 'kewick' sound, while the male's reply is the loud 'twoo' or hooting sound.

PIGEON

The pigeon is the most extraordinary ordinary bird! These greyish, medium-sized birds can be seen as city pests, military heroes or even racing athletes worth huge sums of money each!

CITY LIVING
Pigeons are sometimes called 'flying rats'. Vast numbers gather in busy places, including many of Europe's tourist attractions. They rarely cause disease, but their droppings do cause damage.

PIGEON PIE
Pigeons have been enjoyed as food all over the world, with roast pigeon and pigeon pie being popular in France, Spain and Morocco.

WAR PIGEONS
Homing pigeons are bred to find their way home over long distances, making them excellent messengers. The U.K.'s National Pigeon Service gave more than 200,000 birds to the armed forces. These pigeons delivered vital information from troops on the battlefields near Germany in World War II (1939–1945) and the 'pigeon post' saved many lives.

RACING PIGEONS
With strong chest muscles, pigeons are very fast flyers. This makes them popular birds for sport, in races over distances as far as 1,600km (1,000mi). The sport is now so popular in European countries as well as America and China that top pigeon athletes can be sold for as much as $400,000.

DOCTOR PIGEONS
Pigeons have excellent hearing and can see a greater range of colours than humans. They can also be trained to spot cancer cells in medical tests.

KEY FACTS

Scientific name: *Columba livia*
Size: Length: up to 35cm; wingspan: up to 70cm
Diet: Seeds, berries and small invertebrates. Wild pigeons will eat whatever they can find.
Status: Least concern (wild population decreasing)

Amazing fact: Both male and female pigeons produce a substance called crop milk to feed their chicks. Very few birds have this rare ability; greater flamingos and emperor penguins, as well as pigeons and doves, do.

EURASIAN RED SQUIRREL

Red squirrels play an important part in the life cycle of woodlands. Some of the nuts and seeds they bury underground go on to sprout and grow, keeping the woods alive. Now, changes to their forest homes have begun to make life more challenging.

GREY RAIDERS

Red and grey squirrels can live in the same area quite happily, but when forests are broken up by human developments, food runs short. Then, greys can be more successful. They thrive in urban areas, stealing from bird feeders and gardens.

ACROBAT ANTICS

Sharp claws and a long tail help the red squirrel to climb and balance in the branches. It forages for food, storing some away by burying it underground. When grey squirrels were introduced to the U.K. and Italy, they spread quickly, competing with the reds for food and bringing a virus known as squirrel pox.

CONIFER CONSERVATION

Red squirrels thrive on the little seeds of pine cones, so conifer woodland is vital for their protection. Special feeders and nesting boxes designed for red squirrels help them to settle and breed in new areas of conifer forest.

KEY FACTS

Scientific name: *Sciurus vulgaris*
Size: Head and body length: up to 22cm; tail length: around 18cm
Diet: Nuts, seeds, fruits, buds, flowers, sap, fungi
Status: Least concern (population decreasing)

Amazing fact: The best way to recognise a red squirrel is not by colour, which varies with where they live and when they moult. Reds have ear tufts, and in adults the reds are smaller than the greys.

HOUSE FLY

Originally from Asia, the common house fly is now one of the most widespread insects in the world. Found around human settlements, house flies feed on our waste and are generally considered a pest. However, house fly larvae, called maggots, play an important role in breaking down natural waste.

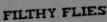

MOVING MEALS

Maggots are high in protein, making a good meal for many insects, birds and reptiles. As adults, house flies have lots of natural predators, so many will be eaten. Luckily for the flies, they are good breeders, with each female fly leaving behind hundreds of the next generation.

MARVELLOUS MAGGOTS

When they first hatch, maggots feed and grow in rotting organic material, such as animal dung or dead bodies. Research is under way to find out how maggots can play a bigger part in removing and recycling waste. In healthcare, maggots are also used to treat wounds. By eating away just the dead flesh, maggots allow cuts to heal cleanly.

FILTHY FLIES

When flies land on human food they spit out saliva that dissolves it before they suck it up. Swatting a fly away from food is very wise, as not only will they defecate (poo) where they land, but they can spread more than 100 different germs on their feet. These are picked up from previous landing sites, which may include the dung or vomit of many other creatures.

KILL OR CURE?

House flies can pass on many diseases, but they do not suffer from the germs they carry. To learn what gives them this immunity, scientists have studied the DNA of the house fly – that's the information in cells that makes all living things look and behave as they do. What scientists have learnt will help with finding new ways to fight diseases and handle waste.

KEY FACTS

Scientific name: *Musca domestica*
Size: Length: up to 8mm
Diet: Animal faeces (poo), garbage, human foods
Status: Not evaluated

Amazing Fact: A female house fly lays batches of around 100–150 white eggs, and may lay more than 500 eggs in her lifetime of just a few days.

GOLDEN EAGLE

Found in areas of Europe, Asia, North America and parts of North Africa, this awesome bird of prey attracts great human interest. Protective laws are guarding golden eagles from the threat of hunting and habitat loss.

SKY DANCING

Golden eagles' hunting range can be as large as 200 square kilometres (77sq mi) of open moorland and mountains, where there is space for their impressive flights and displays. Golden eagles perform fancy air shows known as 'sky dances', circling and swooping to mark their territory and attract a mate.

SYMBOL OF POWER

The golden eagle's power and hunting skills have earned it great respect from many cultures. In falconry – the sport of hunting with a bird of prey – eagles were traditionally flown by kings and emperors, as a sign of their importance.

EAGLE-EYED CONSERVATION

Across Europe, there are thought to be over 9,000 breeding pairs. To monitor eagle numbers, surveys are carried out to record signs of the birds and nesting habits. The surveys also check that babies, called eaglets, hatch and fledge (fly the nest) successfully.

KEY FACTS

Scientific name: *Aquila chrysaetos*
Size: Length: up to 85cm; wingspan: up to 2.2m
Diet: Rabbits, hares, rodents, smaller birds and carrion (dead animals)
Status: Least concern (population stable)

Amazing fact: Golden eagles soar at around 50km per hour, and can free-fall, reaching speeds of 200–300km per hour when hunting.

WILDCAT

Very similar in appearance to pet cats, wildcats are the early ancestors of our tamer companions. European wildcats often look like muscly tabby cats. Found in parts of Europe and Africa, and areas of Asia including India and China, wildcats have a variety of coat colours and patterns according to their location and the season.

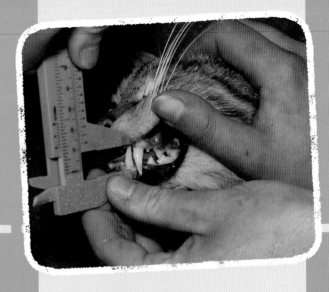

ON THE PROWL

Wildcats mark out their territory with scent markings. They shelter during the day and come out to hunt at dawn, dusk and during the night. Cats' eyes have a special reflective layer that allows them to hunt in very low levels of light. This is also what makes their eyes seem to glow in the moonlight.

This is the Scottish wildcat, the only native species of cat in Britain.

WILD OR FERAL?

Wildcats will often breed with 'feral' or wild-living domestic cats. This makes monitoring the true wildcat population difficult. Sightings are recorded and data is collected where possible, including measurements from the skull and teeth to be compared with other local cats. The purest populations are often in more remote areas.

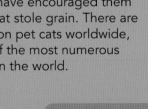

PET POWER

The African wildcat is likely to have been the first wildcat to be tamed. Farmers may have encouraged them to catch the rodents that stole grain. There are now around 600 million pet cats worldwide, making them one of the most numerous mammals in the world.

KEY FACTS

Scientific name: *Felis silvestris*
Size: Head and body: up to 74cm; tail length: 22–37cm
Diet: Small mammals, birds, lizards and spiders
Status: Least concern (population decreasing)

Amazing fact: World War I may have helped wildcats to survive. While landowners were away fighting, the wildcats were not hunted and could recover their numbers.

DONKEY

From miniature donkeys to the enormous American mammoth donkey, there are more than 40 million donkeys in the world today. Descended from the African wild ass, which is now very rare, the hardworking standard donkey has played a vital role in human history.

KEEP CALM AND CARRY ON

For thousands of years, donkeys have helped humans at work. The strength of a donkey allows it to carry heavy loads, pull ploughs, raise water from wells or work mills. In developing countries, donkeys can be vital for people's survival.

ASSES' MILK

Egyptian pharaoh Cleopatra is said to have bathed every day in the milk of donkeys, also known as asses. Donkey milk has been used for its medical qualities and skincare benefits by many cultures, including the Romans.

SAFE SANCTUARY

There are now many donkey sanctuaries across Europe, offering shelter for retired or mistreated animals. The sanctuaries campaign for better welfare conditions for working donkeys and also attract visitors to meet the rescued animals.

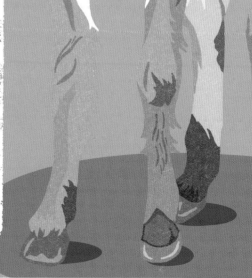

KEY FACTS

Scientific name: *Equus asinus*
Size: Height to shoulder: 1–1.2m
Diet: Vegetation, such as grasses and shrubs
Status: Domestic animal, not evaluated

Amazing fact: Donkeys are intelligent creatures with good memories. They are described as stubborn, but if they refuse to move there is usually a good reason.

EARTHWORM

Charles Darwin, one of the world's greatest natural scientists, studied earthworm behaviour very closely. In his own words, "Worms have played a more important part in the history of the world than most persons would at first suppose."

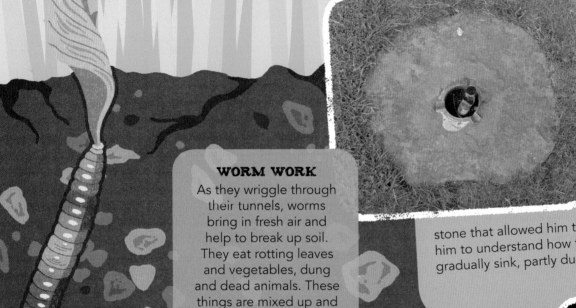

DARWIN'S SINKING STONE

When Darwin noticed that stones in his garden slowly sank into the ground, he realised it was the work of earthworms. He studied the worms closely and built a 'wormstone' – a disc of stone that allowed him to measure this effect. This led him to understand how the stones of ruined buildings gradually sink, partly due to earthworm activity.

WORM WORK

As they wriggle through their tunnels, worms bring in fresh air and help to break up soil. They eat rotting leaves and vegetables, dung and dead animals. These things are mixed up and broken down as they pass through the worm. The waste that leaves the worm at the other end enriches the soil, helping plants to grow. Worms also make a good meal for birds, snails, slugs, snakes and small mammals.

Like recycling machines, worms process organic waste, creating soil perfect for growing plants.

An earthworm at the Yasuni National Park in the Amazon rainforest

GIANT WORMS

Earthworms, or their early relatives, existed long before the mass extinction that wiped out many animals including the dinosaurs around 65 million years ago. Now, there are several thousand different species of earthworm in the world, with some giants reaching as much as 3m (9.8ft) long.

KEY FACTS

Scientific name: *Lumbricus terrestris*
Size: Length: up to about 30cm
Diet: Decaying organic matter from soil, such as animal manure and rotting leaves
Status: Not evaluated

Amazing fact: There are no male or female earthworms. All earthworms have both male and female parts – but it still takes two of them to reproduce.

EUROPEAN BADGER

Widespread across much of Europe, badgers build underground setts in woodland and pasture. Their black-and-white faces are easy to recognise, but their night-time existence keeps them mostly hidden from human life.

READY, GET SETT... STAY

Badgers build underground burrows called setts. Some are small and simple, but others are large and last for several generations. Larger setts have 50–100 entrances and networks of tunnels linking straw-lined chambers. These setts are at risk when towns spread into the country, and many badgers are killed by vehicles when roads are built near their homes.

Badgers can spread diseases, so some may be vaccinated and returned to their setts.

COUNTRYSIDE CHARACTERS

Stories such as *The Wind in the Willows* by Kenneth Grahame have made the badger a much-loved character of the countryside. Nature-watchers enjoy the activity around badger setts, setting up hide-outs and waiting until nightfall to spot them.

BADGERING BADGERS

Badgers are hunted in some countries, including Germany and Finland, but are protected by law in many parts of their range. Badger fur was traditionally used to make shaving brushes because it holds water very well.

KEY FACTS

Scientific name: *Meles meles*
Size: Head and body length: 90cm
Diet: Earthworms, insects, small mammals, birds, reptiles, amphibians, dead animals, nuts, fruits, roots, tubers and fungi

Status: Least concern (population stable)
Amazing fact: Badgers are some of the fastest diggers in the world. Their front paws are like strong shovels, with claws as long as 4cm.

WILD BOAR

This sturdy, adaptable creature has played an important part in human history. Wild boar are the ancestors of the domestic pigs we see on farms today. They have been hunted for food and for sport over thousands of years, but they still survive, and remain a symbol of great strength.

A domestic pig has an average of 10–12 piglets per litter.

MIGHTY ICON

Wild boar appear on swords, shields and coats of arms. They can even be seen in carvings at Göbekli Tepe in southern Turkey, thought to be the oldest temple in the world.

PIG BUSINESS

The ancient Greeks and Romans dined on wild boar, and then in the Middle Ages a roasted boar's head became the centrepiece of Christmas feasts for the wealthy. Today, there are around a billion domestic pigs farmed worldwide, making them one of the most numerous creatures on our planet.

ESCAPE TO THE WILD

In several European countries, farmed boar have escaped and re-settled in the wild, and their numbers are increasing. In their natural environment, boar help to mix up the soil as they forage. They spread seeds in their droppings and help the woodlands to grow. However, when they forage in gardens and farmland, they can cause terrible damage.

STRIPY BABIES

Wild boar tend to live in large groups called sounders. A female makes a nest of twigs, leaves and grasses, where she gives birth to around five to six piglets. Boar piglets have a striped coat up to about four months old, which keeps them camouflaged in the woodland shadows.

KEY FACTS

Scientific name: *Sus scrofa*
Size: Head and body length: 2m; height to shoulder: 1.1m
Diet: Grass, nuts, roots, tubers, insects, small reptiles, carrion (dead animals)

Status: Least concern (population unknown)
Amazing fact: Wild boar can be strong swimmers. They have been spotted swimming in the sea off Italy and Poland.

EUROPEAN RABBIT

All breeds of pet rabbit originally come from the European rabbit – from little dwarf lop-eared bunnies to giants the size of dogs! They have a mixed relationship with humans, and may be treated as a terrible pest, a source of food, or simply as an important part of the countryside.

BREEDING LIKE RABBITS

Rabbits are well known for breeding very quickly and can produce as many as 15–45 babies a year. The rabbits brought by European settlers to Australia spread so quickly that they became a pest. They threatened the native burrowing animals and took over the grazing lands of the sheep.

UPS AND DOWNS

In the Middle Ages, rich landowners kept rabbits for hunting and employed 'warreners' to manage them. By the 18th century, large populations of rabbits in the wild became a popular food for the poor. In the 1950s, a disease called myxomatosis was deliberately released in France to control the rabbit population. It had such a dramatic effect that it quickly killed off large numbers of rabbits across Europe.

HOPPING HELPERS

Across its range, the European rabbit is important for many other species. It is key to the diet of the Spanish imperial eagle and the endangered Iberian lynx. Rabbits are used to train lynx cubs bred in captivity, to prepare them for hunting in the wild.

KEY FACTS

Scientific name: *Oryctolagus cuniculus*
Size: Head and body length: up to 38cm; tail length: 7cm
Diet: Mainly grass, some other flowering plants
Status: Near threatened (population decreasing in its natural range)

Amazing fact: Rabbits' eyes are high up on the sides of their heads, which allows them to see almost all around them – nearly 360°! This helps protect them from predators, such as foxes and birds of prey.

EUROPEAN HONEY BEE

Many people are still unaware of just how important these buzzy little insects are to human life today. Worldwide, they pollinate a wide range of important crops, worth billions of dollars. We depend on them to pollinate around 400 plants, including fruit, cereal crops, vegetables, coffee, tea and even cotton. They also produce nature's liquid gold – honey.

Ancient Egyptian carving of beekeeping at the Tomb of Pabasa in Luxor

FLOWERS TO HONEY

As long as 5,000 years ago ancient Egyptians kept bees for their honey, as we can see from their tomb carvings. Honey bees are likely to have come from Africa, but they are now found worldwide. In Europe, Greece and Hungary have the most per hectare. In the wild they build nests in hollow trees, but will also colonise man-made hives. Bees feed on pollen and nectar from flowers, then store spare nectar in honeycomb structures in their nests. The stored, concentrated nectar is called honey.

A WARNING STING

If threatened, worker bees and queens can deliver a painful sting. When a worker bee stings, it tears its abdomen, leading to its death. The worker bee may have lost its life, but it has protected the other bees by warning off the predator. A special chemical known as a pheromone, which acts like an alarm call to other bees, is also released.

KEY FACTS

Scientific name: *Apis mellifera*
Size: Length: queen: up to 20mm; males: up to 17mm; workers: up to 15mm
Diet: Mainly nectar and pollen
Status: Not evaluated

Amazing fact: In a colony of bees there will be one queen and thousands of female worker bees. The sole function of the males, called drones, is to fertilise the queen's eggs.

This bee is being attacked by a varroa destructor mite.

STAY LOCAL

Local populations of bees produce different flavours of honey, depending on which flowers they collect nectar from. These smaller populations can be threatened by large commercial bee farms.

Beekeeping is a skilled job and requires the right natural environment for a colony to thrive.

BEES IN DECLINE

Several kinds of mites have caused deadly infestations in bee colonies, causing sharp drops in numbers. Recently in North America, bees have been suffering from Colony Collapse Disorder, when large numbers of bees suddenly disappear from collections of beehives (known as apiaries). Without enough workers, a colony will fail. There may be lots of different reasons why bees are in decline, so research continues to find out exactly what has to be done to protect the world's bees.

PESTICIDE PROBLEMS

New pesticides used to control insects on crops may be causing unexpected harm to bees. While these may be safer for humans, further research is showing that they are very likely to cause bees to suffer.

Pollen is collected in 'baskets' on the bees' legs.

EMPEROR DRAGONFLY

A glimpse of the jewel-like blues and greens of an emperor dragonfly flitting across the surface of a lake or pond can be a magical sight. Rarely stopping for long, these active flyers can be an important marker of environmental change, as well as inspiring art with their beauty.

THE MAKING OF A DRAGONFLY

Dragonflies start life as larvae, known as nymphs, that live under water. Nymphs grow and moult through different stages known as 'instars' over two years. The final moult happens out of the water, triggered by a change in the season. On a waterside plant, the nymph sheds its skin one last time to become a dragonfly.

A dragonfly can fly backwards, upside down or hover to grab its next meal.

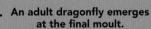

An adult dragonfly emerges at the final moult.

Laying eggs under water

CHALLENGING THE SURVIVORS

As a species, dragonflies have survived ice ages as well as the mass extinction that killed the dinosaurs. Now, human activity brings new challenges. They are found in areas of Europe, Asia, North Africa and the Middle East – but they rely on peaceful, unpolluted waters to survive. They are beginning to spread northwards in some areas, which is an effect of global warming, and shows that other creatures will be affected in time.

CURIOUS CULTURE

Dragonflies and their larvae are a delicacy to eat in some places, including Africa, Asia and the Far East. Their elegance and colour have inspired artists for thousands of years, from ancient Egyptian dragonfly amulets to striking art nouveau jewellery. Across their range, they have many colourful nicknames including Devil's Needle and Water Witch.

KEY FACTS

Scientific name: *Anax imperator*
Size: Length: up to about 8cm
Diet: Larvae eat small pondlife; adults eat insects in flight or land to eat butterflies and moths.
Status: Least concern

Amazing fact: A dragonfly's four wings are each attached to its body by separate muscles, giving it a huge range of movement and the ability to reach speeds of 48km per hour.

BLACK RAT

To humans, the black rat is mostly thought of as a dirty pest – but we only have ourselves to blame. Transported on trade ships from harbour to harbour, black rats have taken advantage of human transport to spread and thrive. Now they have a bad reputation for damaging buildings and spreading deadly diseases.

UNWELCOME GUESTS

Rats will eat almost anything a human eats – and many more revolting alternatives! They thrive in well-populated places, such as busy cities, and can adapt to any place where food is found, including farms and rubbish tips. With sharp front teeth that grow constantly, they do serious damage to wood, bricks and plastic, and will even gnaw through electric cables.

DEADLY DISEASE

Black rats can carry diseases, either via their urine (wee) or via the fleas that feed on their blood. They are linked to many nasty human diseases, including salmonella, listeria and the Black Death – a plague that killed millions of people in the 14th century.

LAB RATS

Laboratory rats (often bred from the brown rat) are used in experiments, to study medicine and behaviour. A rat's brain is similar enough to a human's to allow studies on how our brain works. In some tests, rats are surprising scientists with their intelligence. Testing on animals is considered cruel by many animal rights organisations.

PIED PIPER

In Germany, the story of the Piper of Hamelin is celebrated with street performances. In the story, a rat catcher uses his magic pipe to lure rats away from Hamelin. When the mayor refuses to pay him, the piper leads away the town's children as well.

KEY FACTS

Scientific name: *Rattus rattus*

Size: Head and body length: up to 24cm; tail length: up to 26cm

Diet: Fruit, grain, vegetation, insects and other invertebrates

Status: Least concern (population stable)

Amazing fact: The black rat is an excellent climber, using its very long tail for balance.

RED FOX

The relationship between humans and foxes is not a peaceful one. Traditionally hunted as pests and killed for their fur, foxes are often on the run, but they continue to be successful. An adaptable creature, the red fox is both a hunter and a scavenger. It thrives in towns and the countryside, making the most of any source of food it can find.

TASTY VACCINES

In some parts of continental Europe, foxes are a key carrier of a disease called rabies, which can pass from animals to humans, usually by bites. Scientists are trying to prevent the spread of the disease by giving foxes a vaccine disguised as a tasty treat. Known as baits, these are left for foxes to find in their scavenging areas.

URBAN LIFE

Foxes have spread into urban areas, where they are often spotted in parks and gardens. There they have adapted to steal food from bins and raise litters of cubs near to human homes.

HALTED HUNTING

Foxes have been the target of hunts for thousands of years. Trained hunting dogs called 'scent hounds' were bred to sniff out, chase and kill the fox, and hunting became a popular sport for the wealthy. Fox hunting traditions can be seen in art, culture, and fashion. Fox hunting is now banned or controlled in many European countries because it is thought to be cruel.

KEY FACTS

Scientific name: *Vulpes vulpes*
Size: Head and body length: up to 90cm; tail length: 28–49cm
Diet: Almost anything, including insects, mammals, fruit and human rubbish

Status: Least concern
Amazing fact: Foxes communicate with around 20 different yaps, whines, barks and even a screaming cry.

STOP THIEF

One cheeky urban fox entered the Houses of Parliament in London, U.K., where it fell asleep on a filing cabinet. Others have killed a rare antelope in a zoo in Copenhagen, Denmark, and penguins at Germany's Cologne Zoo!

An urban fox pays a visit to 10 Downing Street, London, home of the British Prime Minister.

Red fox fur varies from light red to dark orange, often with darker legs and some white markings.

ALPINE CHAMOIS

This nimble mountain climber with hooked horns is well adapted to life in the snowy conditions of the Alps. It can run fast, even on steeply sloping ground, and leaps from rock to rock with ease. The fur and hide of the chamois (pronounced 'sham-wah') are used to make a surprising range of products.

SHAMMY LEATHER

The smooth skin of the chamois is particularly good for cleaning and polishing. Known as 'shammy leathers', today these are often made from man-made fabrics designed to feel like chamois hide.

NEWCOMERS ON THE SLOPES

Human disturbance is a growing threat to chamois herds. Males live mostly alone, while females and young live in herds of up to 100. Previously undisturbed in their Alpine habitat, chamois are now facing more human contact as tourism and mountain sports become more popular.

BEARDY HATS

The chamois' tail and the hair from its neck were used as hunting trophies. Traditional hats from Austria and Bavaria are decorated with the tail or the 'Gamsbart', which is the 'beard' of the chamois. More recently, these hats have become tourist souvenirs, often made from the hair of other animals.

The chamois' dark winter fur sheds to lighter brown in summer.

EMPEROR'S GIFT

This picture shows chamois being delivered to New Zealand in 1907. Austrian Emperor, Franz Joseph I, gave the chamois as a gift. Environmental conditions were just right for the chamois to spread quickly.

KEY FACTS

Scientific name: *Rupicapra rupicapra*
Size: Head and body length: up to 1.3m; tail length: up to 10cm
Diet: Grasses and other flowering plants in summer; browses shrubs and trees in winter

Status: Least concern (population unknown)
Amazing fact: Alpine chamois are shrinking! They weigh as much as 25 per cent less than they did 30 years ago, possibly due to climate change.

CAT FLEA

An itchy pet scratching all day usually means one thing – fleas! Unless careful steps are taken to prevent it, any household with pets can face an infestation of fleas. These barely visible insects can be hard to remove, so we go to great effort and expense to protect our pets.

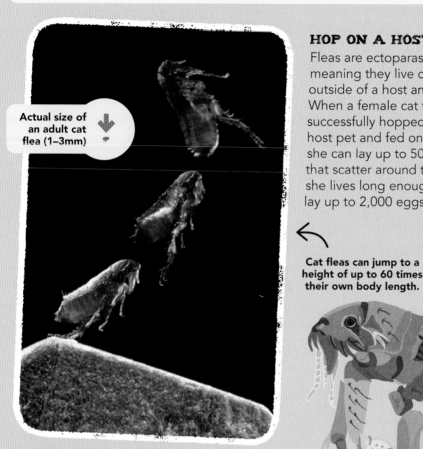

Actual size of an adult cat flea (1–3mm)

← **Cat fleas can jump to a height of up to 60 times their own body length.**

HOP ON A HOST

Fleas are ectoparasites, meaning they live on the outside of a host animal. When a female cat flea has successfully hopped onto a host pet and fed on its blood, she can lay up to 50 eggs a day that scatter around the home. If she lives long enough, she can lay up to 2,000 eggs in total.

CARPET CRITTERS

Flea larvae, shown here in carpet fibres, feed on organic matter around the home. Their main source of food is the blood-filled faeces (poo) of the adult fleas that falls from the coats of the host pets.

MANY AND VARIOUS

The cat flea is the most common domestic flea worldwide, but there are over 2,000 other species. The rat flea is well-known for spreading bubonic plague from rats to humans. Known as the Black Death, this disease killed millions of people in the Middle Ages.

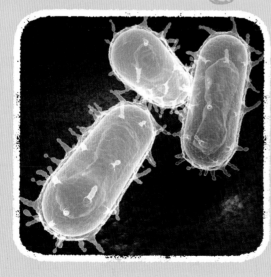

During an outbreak of bubonic plague, flea bites can spread the *Yersinia pestis* bacteria that causes the disease.

KEY FACTS

Scientific name: *Ctenocephalides felis*
Size: Length 1–3mm
Diet: Blood
Status: Least concern

Amazing fact: This tiny creature is thought to be the most successful external parasite on Earth. It prefers cats, but will also feed on other creatures including dogs, rabbits and horses.

AFRICA

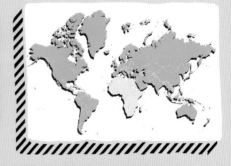

Stretching to the north and south of the equator, Africa is the second largest continent. With hot deserts, savannah plains and tropical rainforests, Africa's habitats suit a rich variety of wildlife, as well as over a billion people. Off the southeast coast lies Africa's largest island, Madagascar – home to hundreds of fascinating species, many found nowhere else on Earth.

PEOPLE AND PLACES

Africa is home to many ethnic groups, each with their own traditions, cultures and languages. In the past, most people lived in small rural communities. Now, many live in cities of more than 20 million such as Cairo and Lagos.

Egypt's Great Pyramid of Giza is the only one of the Seven Wonders of the Ancient World still standing today.

Mother and child of the Maasai people of East Africa

WONDER OF THE WILDERNESS

Africa's natural beauty attracts millions of people each year. The Nile in northeastern Africa is the longest river in the world and the continent also features the Atlas Mountains, the Great Rift Valley and the Sahara Desert. To the east lie some of the world's most impressive wildlife reserves, including the vast Serengeti, meaning 'endless plain'.

Map labels

EUROPE

Mediterranean Sea

Morocco
Algeria
Libya
Egypt
Western Sahara
Mauritania
Mali
Niger
Chad
Sudan
ASIA
Senegal
Burkina Faso
Eritrea
Djibouti
Guinea
The Gambia
Guinea-Bissau
Côte D'Ivoire
Ghana
Nigeria
Central African Republic
South Sudan
Ethiopia
Sierra Leone
Liberia
Togo
Benin
Cameroon
Somalia
Equatorial Guinea
Gabon
Democratic Republic of Congo
Uganda
Kenya
Republic of Congo
Rwanda
Burundi
Tanzania
Indian Ocean
South Atlantic Ocean
Angola
Mozambique
Zambia
Zimbabwe
Madagascar
Namibia
Botswana
South Africa
Malawi
Swaziland
Lesotho

AFRICAN SAVANNAH ELEPHANT

Bigger than their Asian relatives, African elephants are the largest land mammals in the world today. Elephants clear paths through dry woodland and scrub, dig waterholes in dry rivers and spread seeds in their dung. This useful behaviour creates the perfect environment for many other creatures, making the elephant a keystone species for the continent.

FINDING THE FOREST ELEPHANT

There are two species of African elephant: the savannah elephant (shown below) and the forest elephant (shown left), which is smaller with straight tusks and a preference for the shelter of the forest. The two different species need separate conservation plans.

The large ears of the African savannah elephant resemble the shape of the continent.

BEAUTY AND THE BEAST

African savannah elephants use their ivory tusks for many things, including digging for food, water and salt and for self defence. The beauty and value of their tusks puts elephants at great risk from hunters. Ivory has been used for jewellery, decorative items, piano keys and billiard balls. International trade in ivory was banned in 1989, but poachers still hunt elephants.

BIG ATTRACTION

People travel from all over the world to Africa to see the landscape and wildlife. This brings money and opportunities to the local people.

Found south of the Sahara Desert, the elephant is known as one of the 'big five' of animal tourism, along with the lion, rhinoceros, leopard and buffalo.

KEY FACTS

Scientific name: *Loxodonta africana*
Size: Head and body length including trunk: up to 7.5m; shoulder height: up to 3.3m; tail length: 1–1.5m
Diet: Grasses, vegetation, fruits and seeds
Status: Vulnerable (population decreasing)

Amazing fact: Elephants make a range of noises including very low 'infrasonic' sounds. These are too low for humans to hear, but they allow elephants to communicate over very long distances.

WHITE-BACKED VULTURE

With its featherless black head and neck and its hooked beak, the white-backed vulture is a skilled scavenger with a very important role. Feeding on the dead bodies of large animals, it leaves bones clean of rotten flesh, cutting down the spread of disease.

SUDDEN DROP

In 2015, sharp drops in population led to the white-backed vulture being classed as critically endangered. Farmland has spread across their habitat, pushing out their prey. National parks are now sheltering vultures, tagging them and studying their breeding habits to help increase their numbers again.

SKY SEARCH

Vultures are well adapted to scavenging. Soaring in the African skies, they save energy by gliding on warm air currents called thermals. Once they spot a carcass (dead animal), the flock lands to feed together. As many as 500–600 will gather if there is an elephant carcass to feed on.

PYLON PROBLEMS

Vultures usually nest in tall trees, such as acacia. In some areas, vultures will perch or roost in man-made structures, such as pylons and power lines. These extra nesting sites also bring a risk of injury and even electrocution.

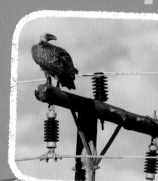

A vulture's hooked beak tears the flesh from bones.

KEY FACTS

Latin name: *Gyps africanus*
Size: Length: up to 94cm; wingspan: up to 2.2m
Diet: Carrion
Status: Critically endangered (population decreasing)

Amazing fact: There has been a very sudden, sharp drop in population for this large scavenger. It is estimated there are 90 per cent fewer birds today than just 55 years ago.

COMMON HIPPOPOTAMUS

The hippopotamus is the third-largest land mammal after the elephant and rhino. During the day, hippos keep cool in water, emerging in the evening to graze on land. The pathways they tread are helpful for other creatures, but damage to the land makes them unpopular with farmers.

RIVER HORSES

The name hippopotamus comes from the ancient Greek for 'river horse'. With eyes, ears and nostrils high up on their heads, hippos can almost completely submerge themselves in the water and still see, hear and breathe. Careful study of the species has shown that hippos' closest living relatives are the aquatic mammals: whales, dolphins and porpoises.

TEETH TROUBLE

Few predators are large enough to threaten an adult hippo, but human hunters are a threat. Despite laws to protect them in many areas, hippos are still killed by poachers for their meat and ivory. After the ban on elephant ivory in 1989, the illegal trade in hippo ivory shot up. Hippos' large canine teeth can measure up to 60cm (24in) in length, making them very valuable to poachers.

DUNG FLINGING

Hippos leave a trail of dung in rivers and lakes, which provides fish and other water life with nutrients from the land. The San people, or Bushmen, tell a folk-tale in which the hippo flings his dung to the land to prove that he has eaten no fish. In keeping with the tale, hippos spin their tails to spray their dung, most likely to mark their territory or attract a mate.

KEY FACTS

Scientific name: *Hippopotamus amphibius*
Size: Head and body length: up to 5m; tail length: 40–45cm; height to shoulder: up to 1.7m
Diet: Grasses, vegetation, crops, occasionally aquatic vegetation and carrion

Status: Vulnerable (population decreasing)
Amazing fact: Hippos startle easily and can be aggressive. They can kill in self-defence, and are among the most dangerous animals in Africa.

AFRICAN LION

The mighty lion is known by many different cultures as the king of beasts. It has become a symbol of nature – wild and powerful – appearing in ancient art, classic literature, and even modern branding. Sadly, despite our love of lions, people are still the species' greatest threat.

MANE EVENT

Everybody recognises the lion, so it is one of the most popular animals to visit, either in its natural environment or in captivity. It is one of the 'big five' of wildlife tourism, bringing much-needed money to Africa's national parks and local people. As apex predators, at the top of the food chain, lions help to control the numbers of zebra, wildebeest and buffalo, keeping the balance of the savannah ecosystem.

INSPIRING ART

Lions appear in carvings, paintings and sculptures in cultures from the ancient to the modern. One of the oldest sculptures in the world, the Great Sphinx of Giza in Egypt, has a human head and the body of a lion. Lions also appear as literary characters, including the Cowardly Lion in *The Wonderful Wizard of Oz* and Aslan in *The Lion, the Witch and the Wardrobe*.

MEET THE RELATIVES

A single population, numbering around 400, of a subspecies called the Asiatic lion lives in India. This endangered animal is now fully protected in the Gir National Park. Disease is a dangerous risk to this limited population. Conservation organisations recommend that some are moved to a second reserve, for better protection against disease.

TREACHEROUS TIMES

The lion population in Africa has suffered a shocking drop over the last 21 years. Lion numbers have almost halved, and there are now fewer than 20,000 left. There are many different reasons for this, all largely caused by humankind. Lions are hunted for sport and killed by farmers who see them as a danger. When parts of their habitat are taken over by farmland, this pushes out the normal prey and brings pesticides. In addition, the meat of wild animals (bushmeat) has become more popular, so humans are also competing with lions for their prey.

HUNTERS TO HELPERS

Lion conservation organisations work together with local people, such as the Maasai in parts of Kenya and Tanzania. Warrior tribes like the Maasai have strong hunting skills and great respect for lions, which are an important part of their culture. Maasai people can track lions and warn herders where lions may attack. This protects the livestock, and the future of the lions too.

A Maasai man photographing lion tracks

KEY FACTS

Scientific name: *Panthera leo*
Size: Head and body length: up to 2.5m; tail length: up to 1m
Diet: Hoofed mammals (including African buffalo, wildebeest and giraffe), also ostrich, reptiles and scavenged meat. Hippos and elephants can be eaten by larger prides of lions.

Status: Vulnerable (population decreasing)
Amazing fact: The lion has the loudest roar of all the big cats. It can be heard as far as 5km away.

CHIMPANZEE

The chimpanzee and the bonobo, or pygmy chimp, are our closest living relatives. Humans share a common ancestor with the chimps and the bonobo that lived around six to eight million years ago. Humans have a fascination with chimpanzees, not just because they look so similar to us, but because they can make and use tools – a skill that people once thought was unique to us.

TOOL TALENTS

Chimps can walk upright, but tend to use their knuckles as well as their feet, known as 'knuckle-walking'. They build nests in the trees at night, but during the day they forage for food. Using sticks and rocks as tools, they dig termites from their nests, crack nuts, scoop up honey and get at hard-to-reach water in the dry season.

UNDERSTANDING CHIMPS

Jane Goodall, a groundbreaking expert on chimpanzees, was the first to discover that they use tools. In 1960, she travelled to the Gombe Stream Reserve in Tanzania, where she began a study of chimps that has lasted more than 50 years. This research has shaped most of what we now understand about chimps' social lives and abilities. She gives chimps names rather than numbers, an example other researchers now follow.

PROTECT AND LEARN

Chimpanzees are recognised as endangered species, and protected in most of their range. Sadly, the laws that protect them are not always respected. Large areas of forest have been cut down, new roads divide the population and illegal hunting continues. Enforcing the laws is the only way we can save chimps from extinction and learn more about this very close relative.

KEY FACTS

Scientific name: *Pan troglodytes*
Size: Head and body length: up to 96cm
Diet: Mainly fruit, also vegetation, fungi and eggs. Insects and mammals, including other monkeys, may also be eaten.
Status: Endangered (population decreasing)
Amazing fact: Most of the information in human cells that makes us who we are – our genes – is almost identical to chimpanzee genes. Humans share 98.8 per cent of chimpanzee DNA. Even with DNA so similar, humans and chimps have around 35 million differences between them.

CHEETAH

The cheetah is the only living member of its scientific group, or genus. All other members of this genus, *Acinonyx*, are now extinct. Slim and light, with black tear-like streaks on its face, the cheetah looks different to other cats, and its survival depends on a very different approach to conservation.

HOME ALONE

Cheetah cubs are at high risk from predators such as lions, hyenas and eagles, and as many as half will be killed. A mother cheetah will have three to five cubs, but to hunt she must leave them alone. To try to keep them safe, she moves the cubs regularly.

CLEVER CONSERVATION

Cheetah numbers have dropped from around 100,000 in 44 countries, to only 12–15,000.

On nature reserves, cheetahs often fail to thrive because of larger predators. Efforts to breed them in captivity have also had a poor success rate.

Careful research has led to a better understanding of cheetahs' breeding patterns. By teaching and sharing this knowledge, conservation organisations are improving cheetahs' chances of survival in captivity and in the wild.

STEALTH AND SPEED

The cheetah has a light build, a long tail and a flexible spine. After creeping as close as possible, it can perform a high-speed chase reaching nearly 90km (56mi) per hour. Occasionally males, particularly brothers, work as a team to catch larger prey such as wildebeest.

SPOT THE DIFFERENCE

The king cheetah is a colour variant of the common cheetah, with stripes down its back. To be marked in this way, a cub must inherit a particualr gene from both its parents. This means king cheetahs are extremely rare in the wild.

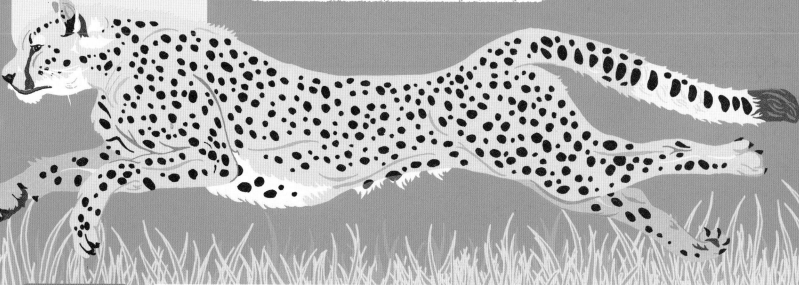

KEY FACTS

Scientific name: *Acinonyx jubatus*
Size: Head and body length: up to 1.4m; tail length: 63–76cm
Diet: Gazelles and small antelope. Cheetahs will also eat the calves of larger hooved mammals and ground-dwelling birds.

Status: Vulnerable (population decreasing)
Amazing fact: Cheetahs do not have good night vision. They mostly hunt during the day, either in the early morning or in the evening, to avoid competing with lions.

LEOPARD

The leopard, with its beautifully spotted coat, is the most widespread of the big cats across Africa and Asia. Sadly, human activities have damaged the leopard population. The future of the leopard and its natural environment now depends on conservation and changing human behaviour.

Fixing a radio tracking collar to an Amur leopard

Like black jaguars, leopards with mostly black fur are known as panthers.

CAREFUL CLIMBERS

Leopards can adapt to various habitats, from jungles to deserts, and will feed on many different animals. To protect their meal from other carnivores, they drag their catch up a tree to eat undisturbed.

TRACKING AND CHANGING

Conservation organisations work hard to gather information about leopards. By tracking them and finding patterns in their behaviour, they hope to teach people how to live alongside leopards peacefully.

BEWARE OF THE HUMANS

The spread of farmland across Africa has reduced the natural territories of leopards and their prey. Humans also bring the threat of hunting. The leopard's beautiful and valuable fur is used in local ceremonies and sold to western countries.

THE AMUR LEOPARD

Many subspecies of leopard are now critically endangered. The world's rarest cat is the Amur leopard, also known as the Far Eastern leopard, with fewer than 70 left. At the Land of the Leopard National Park in Russia, the Amur leopard population is increasing, proving that habitat protection does make a difference.

KEY FACTS

Scientific name: *Panthera pardus*
Size: Head and body length: up to 1.9m; tail length: 64–90cm
Diet: A wide variety of mammals and birds, depending on location

Status: Near threatened (population decreasing)
Amazing fact: These camouflaged hunters are capable of catching a wide range of prey, including young giraffes, that may weigh as much as three times more than the leopard itself.

DESERT LOCUST

The desert locust is usually harmless and lives alone, yet in enormous swarms this insect can cause shocking damage to crops. Scientists now understand why this occurs, but plagues of locusts still cause terrible problems in parts of the world today.

Nymph in solitary phase

TRIGGERING A SWARM

After a drought (a time of very little rain) new rainfall and sudden growth of vegetation can start a chain of events that leads to a locust swarm. Moist ground helps locusts' eggs to hatch. The young hoppers that cannot yet fly crowd together and compete for food. Scientists have discovered that this contact sets off changes in their bodies and their behaviour. Their muscles grow stronger and they even change colour!

ON THE MOVE

A swarm of hungry desert locusts can travel amazing distances. One swarm flew from northwest Africa to Great Britain in 1954, and another travelled from West Africa to the Caribbean in 1988. A single swarm can include around 50–100 billion insects. This hungry crowd will eat most vegetation, including many important crops.

EDIBLE INSECTS

In areas affected by famine, where it is hard to find food and people are hungry, locusts can be an important source of protein. In many African countries, locusts are fried and eaten, or collected and sold to markets.

Adult locust in swarming phase

EARLY WARNING

Once locusts are swarming, they are challenging to stop. Spraying pesticides can work, but causes other problems with the environment. Now, new technology is helping. Monitoring stations and space satellites now gather information to help forecast where and when locusts may breed.

KEY FACTS

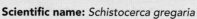

Scientific name: *Schistocerca gregaria*
Size: Length: up to 6cm
Diet: Plants, including grasses and cereal crops
Status: Not evaluated

Amazing fact: Desert locusts can eat about their own weight in vegetation every day. A swarm of 100 billion locusts might eat around 200 million kilograms a day!

NILE CROCODILE

Africa's largest crocodilian, the Nile crocodile, is found in rivers, lakes, freshwater swamps and occasionally in salty waters. As the second largest reptile in the world, this dangerous creature can grow to over 6m (20ft) long and take large prey, including antelope, zebra, wildebeest – and occasionally even humans too.

DANGER BELOW

Hidden in the water like a floating log, the Nile crocodile waits with just its eyes, ears and nostrils above the water's surface. Then, it will make a sudden and unexpected lunge, grabbing its prey with a strong bite and more than 60 sharp teeth.

CROCS VERSUS HUMANS

Hunted for their strong and beautifully patterned skin, Nile crocodile numbers dropped sharply between the 1940s and the 1960s. Crocodile hunting and export is now controlled, but fear of these apex predators still leads to many being killed by local people.

At the top of the food chain, Nile crocodiles will simply take any prey that comes near. The number of attacks on humans each year is unknown, but thought to be in the hundreds. It is hoped this figure will drop, now that people understand more about the crocodile's natural ranges and hunting behaviour.

Perfectly adapted for the water, the Nile crocodile has a streamlined body, webbed back feet and a very powerful tail.

KEY FACTS

Scientific name: *Crocodylus niloticus*
Size: Length including tail: up to 6m
Diet: Young crocodiles feed on aquatic invertebrates, insects, small fish, amphibians and crustaceans. Adults eat fish, turtles, birds and mammals, and will scavenge dead animals too.

Status: Least concern
Amazing fact: A Nile crocodile can open its mouth wide without water rushing down its throat. A special valve allows it to shut off the throat, so it can grab and hold prey under water.

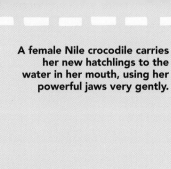

A female Nile crocodile carries her new hatchlings to the water in her mouth, using her powerful jaws very gently.

MIGHTY MUMMIES

The ancient Egyptian god Sobek takes the form of a crocodile, or a human with a crocodile's head. Sobek was a god of fertility, worshipped for his strength and power as well as his ability to protect the weak. In honour of Sobek, Nile crocodiles were mummified by the Egyptians, some with many smaller mummies of their young sewn onto their backs.

SNAPPY FAMILIES

Unlike many other reptiles, female crocodiles will guard their eggs and even roll the eggs gently in her mouth to help the babies hatch. Whether the baby will be a male or female depends on the temperature of the egg. Only if the egg is kept between 31–34°C (88–93°F) will the hatchling be male.

TOP CROC

Crocodiles will bask in the Sun in groups, but there is a strict hierarchy, or order, so the largest, heaviest male will always take the best spot.

WHITE RHINOCEROS

The white rhino is the second largest land mammal, after the elephant. There are five species of rhino: the white and black rhino in Africa, and in Asia the Indian, Javan and Sumatran rhinos. With poor eyesight and large, valuable horns, rhinos are at great risk from poachers, with some species nearing the point of extinction.

MEGA MOWERS

Unlike other rhino species, that prefer to feed on leaves from trees and bushes, white rhinos are like enormous lawnmowers, munching on the savannah grasses. Rhinos are known as 'megaherbivores', and the large amounts they eat help to balance the plant life of the ecosystem, keeping the grasslands just right for many other creatures.

POACHING PERIL

The white rhino's front horn measures around 60cm (2ft) long, but some grow to 150cm (5ft). It is used in traditional Chinese medicine and also to make ceremonial daggers, called jambiyas. Poaching has caused the southern white rhino population to drop sharply, leaving just around 20,000 today.

EXTINCTION IN THE WILD

The northern white rhino is smaller and hairier than its southern relative. It is classed as 'extinct in the wild', and the last few in existence are kept under the protection of armed guards at the Ol Pejeta Conservancy in Kenya. They can no longer breed naturally, but new laboratory techniques offer some hope.

BLACK RHINO

The black rhino is critically endangered and only around 2,400 are left. Despite their names, black and white rhinos are difficult to tell apart by colour. White rhinos are known as 'square-lipped', while black rhinos are 'hook-lipped' because their upper lips curl around leaves and twigs as they feed.

KEY FACTS

Scientific name: *Ceratotherium simum*
Size: Head and body length: up to 4.2m; tail length: up to 70cm; shoulder height: up to 1.8m
Diet: Grasses
Status: Near threatened (population increasing in the southern subspecies)

Amazing fact: A dominant male rhino marks his territory with dung and urine (wee). He will lay piles of dung along the edges of the territory, spraying urine and wiping his horn on bushes and on the ground.

PLAINS ZEBRA

One of the most recognisable animals in the world, the plains zebra has bold black and white stripes and can be seen in large herds on the savannah. Constantly alert to danger, herds stay close together and flee if a predator is spotted. Zebra foals can walk within half an hour of being born – an essential skill for a creature that is the preferred meal of many fierce savannah predators.

EARN YOUR STRIPES

A herd of zebras is made up of a male, called a stallion, with a group of mares (females), called a harem, and their young foals. Other males form separate groups called bachelor herds. To win a female, a male must usually fight her father. Defending her from other males, he will take part in fierce battles to prove his strength.

CLEVER COATS

The exact purpose of the stripes on a zebra's coat is not completely clear. It is likely they have several benefits. No two zebras have exactly the same pattern of stripes, so it is possible that they are used for recognition. As the herd moves, the stripes may also confuse predators, giving individual zebras camouflage in the group. It is also possible that the black and white sections help to keep the zebra cool, as they react to the heat of the Sun in different ways.

FOLLOW THE ZEBRA

Zebras are an important source of food for lions and hyenas, and they also serve the savannah by feeding on tough grass. This encourages fresh growth, which is preferred by many other grazers. In some areas, such as the Serengeti, zebra herds migrate when water runs low, following the rains for new grazing land.

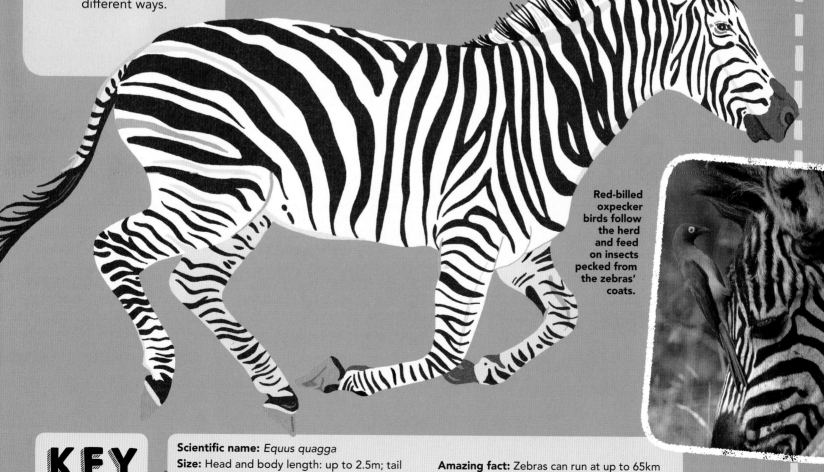

Red-billed oxpecker birds follow the herd and feed on insects pecked from the zebras' coats.

KEY FACTS

Scientific name: *Equus quagga*
Size: Head and body length: up to 2.5m; tail length: 47–57cm; shoulder height: up to 1.4m
Diet: Grasses
Status: Least concern (population stable)

Amazing fact: Zebras can run at up to 65km per hour if under attack, using great stamina and a zig-zag pattern to escape predators such as hungry lions and hyenas.

AFRICAN DUNG BEETLE

Rushing to a freshly laid pile of dung, the African dung beetle forms a dung ball for itself and pushes it away as fast as it can. At a safe distance, it digs a hole and buries the ball. Eggs are laid inside dung balls, so that when the larvae hatch they are surrounded by their food. These important recyclers clear up waste very effectively, taking away the dung of many savannah creatures, and enriching the soil where they store it.

WHO GOES THERE?

Tracking endangered mammals on the savannah can be tricky, but dung beetles provide an essential clue. By trapping flying dung beetles in particular areas, then studying the contents of their guts, scientists can tell which animals' dung they have eaten. The location of rare mammals can then be recorded, even if there is no other sign of them.

To the ancient Egyptians, the dung beetle *Scarabaeus sacer* was sacred. As this little beetle rolled its dung across the ground, it was seen to symbolise the god Khepri, who rolled the Sun across the sky each morning.

WHOSE POO WILL DO?

There are many kinds of dung beetle, including 'dwellers' that live in the dung, 'tunnellers' that bury the dung where they find it, and 'rollers', like the African dung beetle, that take dung balls away. Some prefer the dung of particular animals. When a popular pile of dung is laid – such as an elephant's – many thousands of dung beetles may arrive at the scene.

GUIDING STARS

It's not only humans who use the stars to navigate – amazingly, African dung beetles do too. By climbing on top of its dung ball, the beetle finds its bearings from the stars. It then rolls the ball along the quickest route home. To learn this, scientists blocked the beetles' view with special hats. When they couldn't see the stars, their journeys were winding and uncertain.

These diagrams show the journeys of three beetles rolling dung away from a central pile.

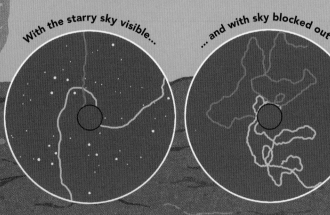

With the starry sky visible...

... and with sky blocked out

KEY FACTS

Scientific name: *Scarabaeus satyrus*
Size: Length: 5mm
Diet: Dung
Status: Not evaluated

Amazing fact: The dung ball made and rolled by an African dung beetle can be 50 times the weight of the beetle itself, or even heavier.

STIR IT UP

To feed, a flamingo bends its head down until its bill is upside down in the water. Kicking with its feet, the flamingo stirs up algae and small water creatures to eat. Then, it swings its head through the water, trapping food in its bill and swallowing it. As the flamingo feeds, its tongue moves backwards and forwards, sucking in and pushing out water like a pump.

Flamingos' feathers take on their pink shade due to colour pigment in their food.

GREATER FLAMINGO

Balanced on one leg, preening its bright pink feathers, the flamingo is a remarkable and iconic bird. These bottom-feeding birds are long-living and adaptable, but climate change brings new threats to their wetland habitats. Performing fancy displays, sometimes in spectacular group formation, flamingos are the ballerinas of the animal world.

MUDDY NESTS

Flamingos lay a single egg on a mound of mud, stones and feathers. Their colonies can number thousands, or even hundreds of thousands, so they may not appear to be a threatened species. However, if food is scarce, flamingos may completely abandon a nesting site. Pollution and global warming threaten their habitat, and wetlands are often drained to create agricultural land.

WHY ONE LEG?

In mudflats and shallow lagoons along the coast, flamingos gather in large colonies, all curiously poised on one leg. This has puzzled scientists, who have wondered if it may be to rest one leg at a time, or perhaps to speed up escape in case of danger. In fact, studies suggest that flamingos may stand on one leg partly in order to keep warm. By keeping one leg tucked up against its body, a flamingo can save some of the heat that would be lost if it had both legs in water for long periods of time.

BREEDING BALLET

When choosing a mate, flamingos will march together in a group, performing a 'head flag' dance, stretching upwards and twisting their heads from side to side. They will also perform movements known as 'wing salutes' and 'twist preen' actions to attract a mate.

KEY FACTS

Scientific name: *Phoenicopterus roseus*
Size: Height: up to 1.5m; wingspan: up to 1.7m
Diet: Small crustaceans and algae give the flamingo its colour; it also feeds on molluscs and worms.

Status: Least concern (population increasing)
Amazing fact: Flamingos live for about 20–30 years, or often longer in captivity. The oldest greater flamingo on record lived to over 83 years old.

RETICULATED GIRAFFE

Tallest of all the animals in the world, the giraffe is an icon of the savannah. These gentle giants have always fascinated humankind, but now science is helping us to understand more about them. Found in eastern Africa, the reticulated giraffe's name comes from the net-like pattern, called reticulation, that creates the striking brown and white patterns of its coat.

STAND TALL AND GET SPOTTED

The giraffe is an important part of Africa's culture and heritage, as well as an icon of the world's wildlife. Conservation organisations are busy raising awareness about giraffes and their natural habitat. They are monitoring the numbers for each species and recording breeding patterns, as well as encouraging education and eco-tourism.

RAINFOREST RELATIVE

A close relative of the giraffe, the okapi lives in the rainforest of the Democratic Republic of Congo. It has a long neck like a giraffe, but the markings on its bottom and legs look more like the stripes of a zebra. This secretive animal was first identified in 1901, and is now endangered because of human threats to its forest range.

GIANT STEPS

At almost 5m (16ft) tall, the giraffe's awesome height allows it to keep watch over the savannah and feed at levels other animals can't reach. An adult giraffe has few predators and can deliver a powerful kick or run at up to 50km (31mi) per hour to escape danger. The downside of a giraffe's impressive height is that lying down or even bending to drink can put it at great risk from a lion attack.

There are fewer than 8,700 of these reticulated giraffes in the world, and other species have even lower numbers.

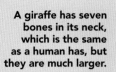

A giraffe has seven bones in its neck, which is the same as a human has, but they are much larger.

SAVANNAH SURVIVAL

Young giraffes, called calves, are targeted by predators such as hyenas, lions and leopards, and around half of those born will be killed before they reach six months old. Human threats, such as illegal poaching and expanding agricultural land, make life even more difficult.

Maasai giraffe coat pattern

WHEN ONE BECOME FOUR

There are currently only around 100,000 giraffes in Africa. Recent studies have revealed that instead of just one species, there are four separate species living in different areas: the reticulated giraffe (shown in the main picture here), the southern giraffe, the northern giraffe and the Maasai giraffe. Each of these look different and they are not known to cross breed in the wild. Now we understand this, protecting the remaining giraffes is more important than ever.

SUCCESS STORY

The Lewa Wildlife Conservancy in Kenya has been so successful protecting animals that there are enough for some to be moved to new protected areas. This includes relocating Rothschild's giraffes (a rare type of northern giraffe). Lewa features on the Green List – a selection of the most valuable protected areas on the planet according to the International Union for the Conservation of Nature.

KEY FACTS

Scientific name: *Giraffa reticulata*
Size: Head and body: up to 4.8m; tail length: 76cm–1.1m
Diet: Leaves, especially from acacia trees
Status: Not yet evaluated (population decreasing)

Amazing fact: A giraffe rips the leaves from trees with a black tongue that measures about 45cm long. Thick saliva protects the mouth and tongue from thorns.

MOUNTAIN GORILLA

The gorilla is the largest of the great apes. Just over 110 years ago, the subspecies known as the mountain gorilla was discovered. Since then, human activity has brought it close to extinction. Just in time, conservation efforts are slowing down the mountain gorillas' alarming drop in numbers.

EARNING TRUST

There are around 4,680 eastern gorillas in Africa – of which only about 880 are the subspecies known as the mountain gorilla. In the Virunga volcano region, mountain gorillas have become familiar with conservation workers. This is called habituation and can allow gorillas to be treated for illnesses and injuries. Eco-tourists also enjoy visiting the area, to see the conservation work in action.

MEET THE FAMILY

A group of gorillas, known as a band or troop, is led by a dominant male called a silverback. Female gorillas usually have one baby at a time, and care for them for as long as four years before another is born. The silverback leads his troop to feeding areas and defends it fiercely against attackers.

LAW AND THE JUNGLE

Laws protect gorillas from hunting and trade, but they still face great danger. In the Democratic Republic of Congo, their habitat is destroyed for farmland, timber and mining. Fighting amongst the people of the region adds to the threat. The Great Ape Survival Project (GRASP), established by The United Nations Environment Programme (UNEP), aims to protect our close relatives with worldwide support.

At the Virunga National Park, guards use satellite navigation devices to record gorilla locations.

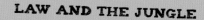

KEY FACTS

Scientific name: *Gorilla beringei beringei*
Size: Head and body: up to 1.2m
Diet: Stems, leaves, bark and occasionally ants. Gorillas' favourite foods include wild celery, bedstraw, nettles, thistles and bamboo shoots.

Status: Critically endangered (population trend unknown)
Amazing fact: The pattern of wrinkles on a gorilla's nose is unique to each one and is known as a 'nose print'. Conservation workers use photos and sketches of gorillas' noses to keep track of individuals.

AFRICAN MALARIA
MOSQUITO

This tiny fly is one of the biggest killers of humans of all time, because of a parasite it can carry. A bite from a mosquito can pass on the parasite that causes malaria, a deadly disease that kills hundreds of thousands of people every year. Scientific research has helped us to understand much more about how this little insect spreads disease, but the battle to prevent it continues.

KILLER BUGS

Globally, malaria kills around 800,000 people every year, with most cases occurring in Africa, particularly in young children. To imagine these shocking numbers, the impact is described as equal to losing seven jumbo jets full of children every day. In Africa during the rainy season, areas of standing water are perfect for the insects to breed and live long enough to spread the parasites that cause malaria.

BLOOD SUCKERS

A mosquito goes through four different stages in its lifecycle, starting out as an egg, then living in water as a larva (pictured), before becoming a pupa and finally a flying adult. It is only the adult female mosquitos that feed on human blood and can spread a range of diseases including malaria.

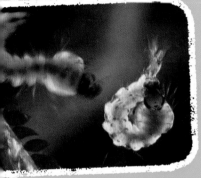

Mosquito larvae

FINDING THE ANSWER

World health organisations have made huge improvements in preventing malaria. Many countries are now malaria-free and the disease is treatable if caught early. New research and education are vital parts of the battle against this tiny but mighty threat.

Homes are sprayed with insecticide and beds are fitted with nets for protection.

Female mosquitos have long tube-like mouthparts that can inject saliva at the same time as drinking blood. The saliva stops the blood from clotting and causes an allergic reaction in most people, so an itchy red bump appears.

Actual size of a female mosquito

KEY FACTS

Latin name: *Anopheles gambiae*
Size: Average wing length: up to 4.4mm
Diet: Males and females eat plant sugars, but the female also feeds on blood.

Status: Not evaluated
Amazing fact: The female's needle-like mouthparts are flexible, so that once they've pierced the skin, they can be moved around inside to find a vein.

RING-TAILED LEMUR

The amazing island of Madagascar is home to the striking ring-tailed lemur. Fossil discoveries show that lemur-like creatures lived in mainland Africa around 60 million years ago and crossed over to Madagascar shortly after. As the island has fewer predators than the mainland, lemurs thrived there and have become an icon of the island.

YOGA LEMURS

Ring-tailed lemurs have several favoured positions that make them very appealing to wildlife watchers. They are often seen in a yoga-like pose, sunbathing with their tummies facing the Sun to soak up the rays. Lemurs live in very social groups and their young are always born around September, when the supply of food on the island is at its best.

MARVELLOUS MADAGASCAR

Madagascar is the fourth-largest island in the world, located in the Indian Ocean, off the coast of southeast Africa. Much of the plant and animal life of this unique island is found nowhere else in the world. In this natural paradise, the ring-tailed lemur's biggest enemies include snakes, birds of prey, the fosa (a mammal related to the mongoose) and, of course, humans.

STINK FIGHT!

To compete for a female, male ring-tailed lemurs will rub their tails with scent from glands in their wrists and shoulders, then shake their tails at each other to waft the smell. The winner is the last to back away from the stink fight, which can last up to an hour.

TROUBLE IN PARADISE

The ring-tailed lemur is a primate – one of a group of mammals that includes humans, apes and monkeys. It has a varied diet and is adaptable, but may still face extinction because its forest home is being destroyed to make charcoal and create space for livestock. Laws have made hunting lemurs a crime, but poachers are still a great risk. Protecting the Madagascan national parks is the only way to safeguard their future in the wild.

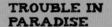

KEY FACTS

Scientific name: *Lemur catta*
Size: Head and body length: up to 46cm; tail length: up to 63cm
Diet: Fruits, leaves, bark, sap, flowers and herbs. The kily tree or tamarind may make up about half of their diet.

Status: Endangered (population decreasing)
Amazing fact: Lemurs are much more intelligent than originally thought, and have surprised scientists with their ability to learn patterns and copy them to earn rewards.

SERENGETI WHITE-BEARDED WILDEBEEST

GREATEST SHOW ON EARTH

The mass movement of migrating animals across the Serengeti, including millions of wildebeest, gazelle, and zebra, is called the 'greatest show on Earth'. This has become popular with eco-tourists, particularly at the crossings of the Grumeti and Mara rivers, where crocodiles lie in wait.

With a population of around 1.3 million, the yearly migration journey of the Serengeti white-bearded wildebeest is one of nature's most amazing spectacles. Roaming the grasslands of eastern Africa, they must drink every few days and feed on fresh grass. When the dry season comes, they set off in search of new feeding areas.

A BEEST FEAST

Wildebeest make an important meal for lions, leopards, cheetahs, crocodiles, hyenas and wild dogs. Younger and weaker members of the herd are targeted. In the breeding season, as many as 400,000 calves are born within a month. Newborn calves must be on their feet and running with the herd within minutes to avoid being caught and eaten.

NEW GENERATIONS

Photographs of the mass migration show so many wildebeest that it may seem as if the population is at no risk. However, as humans spread into wild areas, we change the natural habitat and create dangerous threats. Fences and road links interrupt the migration across the Serengeti. This puts future generations at risk, and without the wildebeest, the ecosystem itself would suffer.

KEY FACTS

Scientific name: *Connochaetes mearnsi*
Size: Shoulder height: up to 1.2m
Diet: Grass
Status: Least concern (population stable)

Amazing fact: Wildebeest are among the top ten fastest animals on Earth, capable of reaching speeds of 80km per hour. With great stamina too, they can often outrun predators such as lions and leopards that can only chase prey over short distances.

PANTHER CHAMELEON

Panther chameleons are among the most colourful creatures in the world. They can be found in a spectacular range of colours and patterns, with males displaying jewel-like blues and greens and females showing startling oranges and reds when they are ready to breed. It is little surprise that these show-stopping reptiles have great appeal to humans. They are icons of Madagascar, where they thrive in forest areas around the coasts of this wildlife haven.

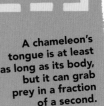

A chameleon's tongue is at least as long as its body, but it can grab prey in a fraction of a second.

RAINBOW ISLAND

The kaleidoscope of colours displayed by this species is affected by a variety of things including light, temperature and how they feel. Chameleons can change colour rapidly when these factors change. Panther chameleons show particular colours and patterns depending on where they come from in Madagascar.

MINI MARVELS

Madagascar is home to around half of the world's chameleon species, currently numbering around 202 with still more being found. A recently-discovered species called *Brookesia micra* lives on the Madagascan island of Nosy Hara and is the smallest ever to be found, measuring just 3cm (1in) in total.

KEY FACTS

Scientific name: *Furcifer pardalis*
Size: Length including tail: up to 50cm
Diet: Insects
Status: Least concern (population stable)

Amazing fact: A chameleon's eyes can swivel around and move independently of each other, so it can see almost 360° and in two directions at once.

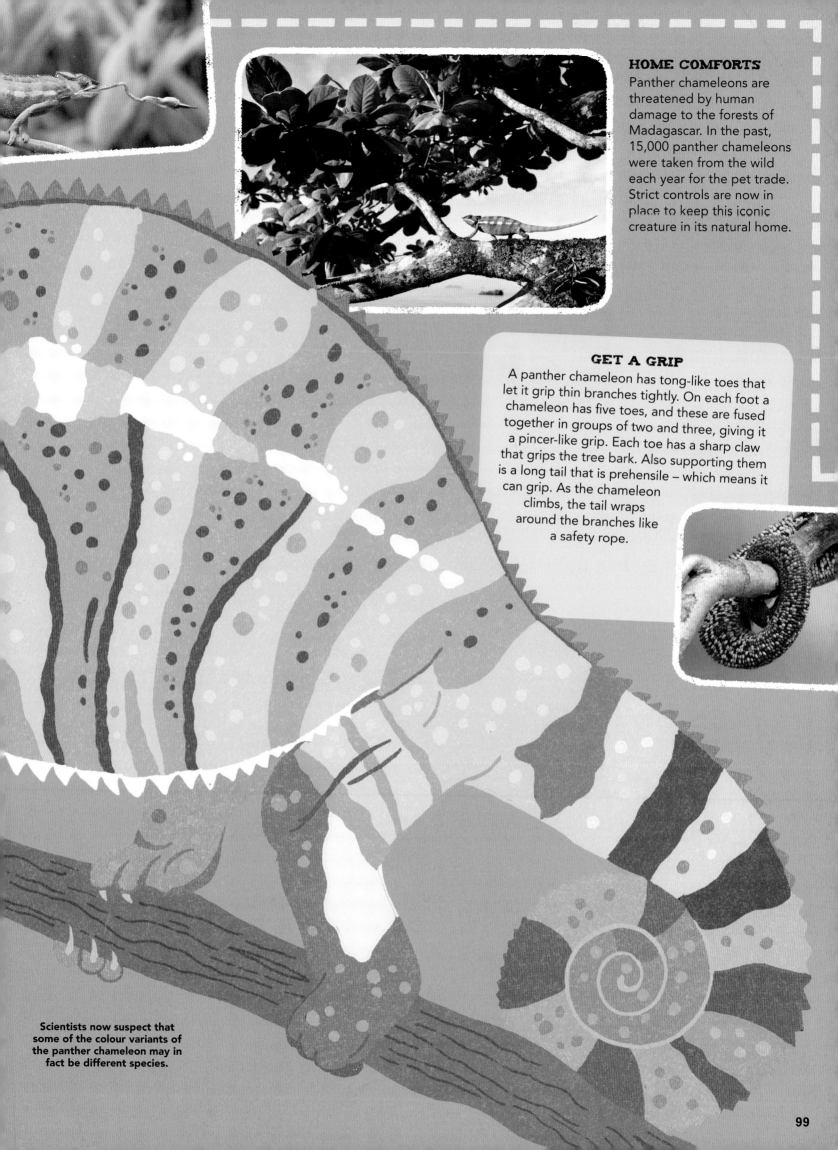

HOME COMFORTS

Panther chameleons are threatened by human damage to the forests of Madagascar. In the past, 15,000 panther chameleons were taken from the wild each year for the pet trade. Strict controls are now in place to keep this iconic creature in its natural home.

GET A GRIP

A panther chameleon has tong-like toes that let it grip thin branches tightly. On each foot a chameleon has five toes, and these are fused together in groups of two and three, giving it a pincer-like grip. Each toe has a sharp claw that grips the tree bark. Also supporting them is a long tail that is prehensile – which means it can grip. As the chameleon climbs, the tail wraps around the branches like a safety rope.

Scientists now suspect that some of the colour variants of the panther chameleon may in fact be different species.

ASIA

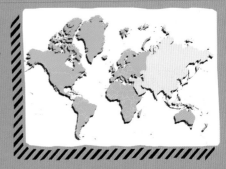

The biggest continent on Earth, Asia is an incredible 44.6 million square kilometres (17.2 million sq mi), stretching from the Arctic Circle in the north to past the equator in the south. It is a land of variety and extremes, with both the highest point on Earth, Mount Everest, and the lowest, at the Dead Sea.

POPULATION EXPLOSION

With a population of above four billion, over half the people in the world live here – more than all the other continents combined. China and India are the most populated countries in the world, each with well over a billion people.

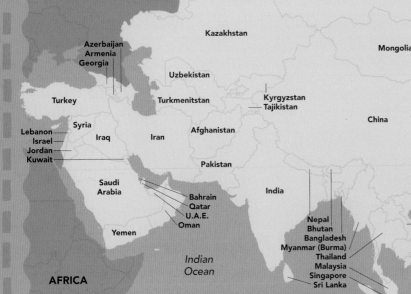

Tokyo, Japan

Built over 2,000 years ago, the Great Wall of China is one of the longest man-made structures in the world.

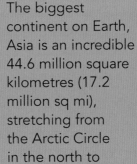

Laptev Sea

Russia

EUROPE

Kazakhstan

Mongolia

Azerbaijan
Armenia
Georgia

Uzbekistan

Turkey

Turkmenitstan

Kyrgyzstan
Tajikistan

China

Syria

Lebanon
Israel
Jordan
Kuwait

Iraq

Iran

Afghanistan

North
Korea

Japan

South
Korea

Saudi
Arabia

Pakistan

India

Bahrain
Qatar
U.A.E.
Oman

Yemen

Nepal
Bhutan
Bangladesh
Myanmar (Burma)
Thailand
Malaysia
Singapore
Sri Lanka

Laos
Vietnam
Cambodia

Taiwan

Philippines

*Pacific
Ocean*

*Indian
Ocean*

AFRICA

Indonesia

HIMALAYAN HEIGHTS

Sprawling east to west from Afghanistan to Myanmar (Burma), the Himalayan mountain range has many of the world's tallest peaks, including Mount Everest. This vast natural barrier plays an important role in the different climates of the continent.

The Himalayas

CHANGING LANDSCAPES

Southeast Asia has some of the fastest-changing landscapes in the world. Where cities, agriculture and industry have spread, natural ecosystems have suffered. In Indonesia, less than half the original forest now remains, and deforestation continues.

OCEANIA

BORNEAN ORANGUTAN

With a name meaning 'person of the forest', this characterful great ape is our close relative. Orangutans once covered a large range across the rainforests of Southeast Asia. Sadly, they are now found on only two islands, where they are icons of wildlife conservation.

ISLAND COUSINS

The islands of Borneo and Sumatra were once connected, but as rising sea levels separated them, the orangutan population was split in two and eventaully evolved into two different species. The total number of these critically endangered animals is at most around 81,000, and their future relies on careful conservation.

A new palm oil plantation

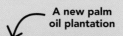

FORESTS UNDER FIRE

Orangutans could face extinction in the wild in as little as ten years. Vast areas of rainforest are destroyed for palm oil plantations. Palm oil is used in thousands of everyday items. Demand for it is so high that the industry continues to spread into the rainforest. In just 20 years, around 90 per cent of the orangutans' habitat has been destroyed.

KEYSTONE CREATURES

Without new generations of orangutans, many forest trees and plants would not grow. Some seeds will only germinate when they have passed through the digestive system of these native primates. Today, these intelligent great apes attract large numbers of visitors. This brings money to the area and spreads awareness of the risks to their jungle home.

LIFE IN THE TREES

Orangutans are the largest tree-dwelling mammals in the world. They find almost everything they need among the branches, and rarely come down to the forest floor. They drink water that collects in the leaves and eat a wide range of different fruits.

KEY FACTS

Scientific name: *Pongo pygmaeus*
Size: Head and body length: up to 97cm
Diet: Mainly fruit
Status: Critically endangered (population decreasing)

Amazing fact: A male orangutan has strong arms with an impressive arm span of around 2m. He uses his weight to sway on a branch, swinging further and further until he can move easily to a nearby tree.

ASIAN ELEPHANT

Not as large as the African elephants that roam the savannah, Asian elephants have smaller ears and often lack tusks. Their strength and intelligence has made them popular as working animals, and they are very important in the culture of Asia. Today, the relationship between humans and elephants is facing new challenges, as we compete for land and food.

NOSY BUSINESS

An elephant's trunk is a useful tool. Besides being used to smell, breathe, and produce sound, it is used to collect food and water. It has around 100,000 muscle fibres and can hold up to 4 litres (7 pints) of water, which elephants enjoy spraying into their mouths or over themselves like a shower.

MUCK SPREADERS

When elephants eat crops, they are often killed or injured by farmers. Elephant conservation depends on teaching about the important role elephants play in their environment. Elephant dung, which they can produce up to 18 times a day, creates very fertile land and spreads many seeds, helping plants to grow and other animals to thrive.

Orphaned elephant calves are raised at a conservation facility until they can be released into the wild.

DISAPPEARING GIANTS

Traditionally, the size and strength of elephants made them important as working animals. Over the last three generations, Asian elephant numbers have dropped by at least half. Where more than 100,000 elephants once lived happily, there are now only about 40–50,000. Despite laws to protect them, elephants are still hunted for meat, leather and ivory.

Elephant riders known as 'mahouts' can build a strong bond with their working elephants.

KEY FACTS

Scientific name: *Elephas maximus*
Size: Length: head and body (including trunk): up to 6.4m; tail length: 1.2–1.5m
Diet: A variety of grasses and other flowering plants
Status: Endangered (population decreasing)
Amazing fact: Males with long tusks are known as 'tuskers' and others without them are called 'makhnas'. The female Asian elephant's tusks, called 'tushes', can rarely be seen beyond the upper lip.

Some Asian elephants have markings that look like pink freckles. This is caused by the skin losing colour, known as depigmentation.

ELEPHANT WORSHIP

Elephants are important creatures in many religions including Hinduism and Buddhism. The Hindu god Ganesh has the head of an elephant and is worshipped for the ability to remove obstacles and create fresh beginnings.

INDIAN PANGOLIN

This very unusual creature is the only mammal with scales. The scales are made of keratin, the same as human hair and nails, and their strength protects the pangolin from predators. However, because these scales are believed to have healing qualities, they have also made the pangolin a popular target for hunters, putting the population at great risk.

A young pangolin is carried on its mother's back or tail until it can feed and explore on its own.

ON A ROLL

With its strong claws and long, sticky tongue, the pangolin feeds from termite mounds and ant nests. To defend itself from biting ants, a pangolin closes its nostrils and ears as well as its eyes, while its tongue roots out the insects from their nests. If threatened, it rolls up into a tight ball, relying on the movable scales to protect its softer underside.

THE SCALE TRAIL

Indian pangolins are killed in their thousands by poachers. Their scales are used whole and powdered in traditional Asian medicines that are believed to pass on the strength of this protective armour. This trade is now illegal, but it may have affected more than a million pangolins since 2000. The future of the pangolin depends on the laws being enforced properly.

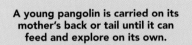

KEY FACTS

Scientific name: *Manis crassicaudata*
Size: Head and body length: up to 75cm; tail length: up to 45cm
Diet: Mainly termites and ants
Status: Endangered (population decreasing)

Amazing fact: The pangolin's long, sticky tongue can be around 25cm long.

ONCE BITTEN

A male Komodo dragon can weigh up to around 100kg (220lbs) and may be even heavier because he can eat as much as 80 per cent of his own weight in meat. These apex predators have venom glands in their jaws, so if their bite alone does not kill the prey, then the venom will.

KOMODO DRAGON

As its name suggests, this awesome lizard resembles the mythical dragons of legend. The Komodo dragon doesn't breathe fire, but it is the largest lizard on Earth, capable of killing large, hoofed mammals. Despite its monstrous reputation, this venomous carnivore now attracts thousands of tourists keen to see dragons in the wild.

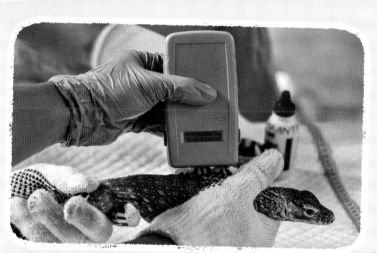

Testing a microchip to monitor a baby Komodo dragon

ISLAND EXPEDITION

Komodo dragons are found on the island of Komodo in Indonesia as well as some of its neighbouring islands. In 1926, after hearing reports of a gigantic, dragon-like reptile, the American Museum of Natural History supported an expedition led by W. Douglas Burden. He returned with 12 preserved and two live Komodo dragons, stirring up a fascination with the creature that continues today.

MIRACLE BIRTHS

In captivity, female Komodo dragons have laid eggs that have successfully hatched with no males around. These 'miracle' births have fascinated scientists. The amazing ability to have babies with no father at all may be the reason this species has survived so long.

This giant reptile attracts around 18,000 visitors a year to Indonesia.

KEY FACTS

Latin name: *Varanus komodoensis*
Size: Length including tail: up to about 3m
Diet: Mainly hoofed mammals and carrion, or almost any other meat (including other Komodo dragons)
Status: Vulnerable

Amazing fact: Komodo dragons have thrived in Indonesia for millions of years, but were not described and studied by scientists until 1912, probably due to their remote location. With only 3,000–5,000 now in existence, there is still a lot to learn.

GIANT PANDA

Probably the most iconic of all endangered species, the panda is much-loved and globally recognised. Threatened by hunting, dramatic habitat loss and climate change, the panda's future looked very uncertain. Thankfully, it has become a conservation success story, as the pandas' rapid drop in numbers has been halted by the efforts of charities and conservation organisations.

CHEW, CHEW, BAMBOO

Pandas are very specialised feeders, surviving almost entirely on bamboo. As a food, bamboo is low in protein and pandas must eat around 12kg (26lbs) per day to keep up their energy levels.

LIMITED LARDER

Pandas are well adapted to their environment. Bamboo was widespread and few other creatures competed for it. If the bamboo died out in one area, their habitat was large enough for pandas to move to a new area. Now that human activity has broken up their habitat, their limited diet puts them at greater risk.

A key sign in the search for pandas is their dung.

COUNTING PANDAS

There may be as few as 1,864 pandas and their babies in the wild. They are secretive creatures, so counting them is challenging. National surveys have been carried out over ten years, covering millions of hectares of land. Pandas have the digestive system of a carnivore (meat-eater) so the bamboo they eat is not digested very well. This makes their dung easy to recognise, because it looks like crushed bamboo! As pandas poo around 40 times a day, it is an important way of recording where they have been.

BETTER BREEDING

Forest reserves now give pandas a safe habitat, and killing a panda can lead to a prison sentence under Chinese law. Between these protected areas, special links are in place to make sure pandas can mix for breeding.

Pandas are often thought to be poor breeders, not very interested in reproducing. Now, much more is understood about their breeding habits, which makes captive breeding more successful. Females are only ready to breed for a short time, once a year, and two cubs are usually born.

DOUBLING UP

Newborn pandas are extremely tiny, weighing just 100–200g (3–7oz). One of the two cubs will often be abandoned, as the mother cannot produce enough milk for both. In China, conservationists have been removing the abandoned cubs, and sharing out their time with their mother. By doing this, both cubs receive the mother's milk and care, greatly helping their chances of survival.

KEY FACTS

Scientific name: *Ailuropoda melanoleuca*
Size: Head and body length: up to 1.8m; tail length: 10–16cm
Diet: Bamboo (a tiny part of a panda's diet is made up of other plants and small mammals)

Status: Vulnerable (population increasing)
Amazing fact: A giant panda has very strong jaws and broad, flat molar teeth, around seven times larger than human teeth. It uses these teeth for around 12 hours a day, chewing bamboo.

INDIAN PEAFOWL

The tail feathers of the male peafowl, known as a peacock, create one of nature's most impressive displays. In shiny blues and greens, his tail forms a fan shape, quivering to show off the large eye-shaped markings. Inspiring art, religion and culture all over the world, the peafowl is a symbol of beauty and wealth.

SCREAMS IN THE FOREST

A peacock's train can be over 1.5m (4.9ft) long, but will be shed each year after the breeding season. Female peafowl, called peahens, do not have a long train and showy colours. Peafowl are very noisy birds, making sudden, loud 'kee-ow' screams.

The fancy feathers on peafowls' heads are called crest feathers.

FEATHERY FORTUNE

The largest member of the pheasant family, the Indian peafowl is the national bird of India. Legends describe them as snake-killers and while some think peacock feathers bring good fortune, others believe they bring bad luck.

ORNAMENTAL BIRDS

These ornamental birds are often kept at temples, estates and parks. In Hinduism, Indra, the god of thunder, rains and war, is shown in the form of a peacock. The Hindu god Krishna is always shown wearing a peacock's feather, said to be a gift from the king of peacocks for his beautiful flute playing.

The colourful eye-shaped markings, called 'ocellus', are believed to represent the universe.

KEY FACTS

Scientific name: *Pavo cristatus*
Size: Length: up to 2.3m, including up to 1.6m of tail (males); wingspan: up to 1.6m
Diet: Seeds, fallen fruits and invertebrates
Status: Least concern (population stable)

Amazing fact: When a peacock quivers his tail, it makes a sound so low that humans can't hear it. This carries to other peafowl, even before they see the peacock's impressive feather display.

RED JUNGLEFOWL

From the jungles of Southern Asia, red junglefowl are likely to be the ancestors of the domestic chickens we know so well today. Since people first began to bring forest birds into their villages for eggs, the popularity of keeping fowl has spread across the globe. Today, there is a huge industry supplying our enormous appetite for chicken meat and eggs.

Male red junglefowl

Female

With so many domestic chickens in the world, the pure wild junglefowl are now very rare.

WILD AT HEART

The handsome male red junglefowl has gold, brown, red and orange feathers and a tail in shades of shiny metallic green and blue. The female is a much paler brownish gold. Unlike domesticated chickens, the true wild red junglefowl has white patches on either side of its head and greyish feet. Wild males also have an 'eclipse moult', when the colourful neck plumage is replaced with dark feathers and the long tail feathers fall out.

CRACKING EGGS

Around 8,000 years ago, people began to keep wild fowl, possibly for a sport called cockfighting. When junglefowl are well fed, they lay more eggs, so the first fowl-keepers would soon have enjoyed the benefits of caring for their birds.

COUNTING CHICKENS

Today, there are around 19 billion chickens in farms and homes all over the world, kept for their meat and eggs. Domestic hens are bred to lay around 80 times more than their ancestors, and around 60 million tons of eggs are laid each year. This has led to animal welfare organisations campaigning for 'free range' farming, where chickens are kept more naturally.

KEY FACTS

Scientific name: *Gallus gallus*
Size: Length: up to 71cm; wingspan: up to 51cm
Diet: Seeds, fallen fruit and insects
Status: Least concern (population decreasing)

Amazing fact: During the breeding season in spring, a female red junglefowl will lay an egg a day, which each take 21 days to hatch out. She will only lay around 15 eggs a year.

WILD BACTRIAN CAMEL

There are more than two million domestic Bactrian camels in Central Asia, but the original wild population is treated as a separate species. Limited to as few as around 600 in China and 800 in Mongolia, the wild species has become an urgent conservation concern.

Thick eyelashes and narrow nostrils help to keep sand away, while the camels' broad feet spread out to stop them sinking into the shifting ground.

NOMADIC NEEDS

The nomadic people of the Gobi Desert relied on Bactrian camels for their meat, wool and milk. Strong, hardy creatures, the camels also provided transportation for the nomads and their possessions. Today, they are still a vital part of nomadic life. Camels are marked with paint or textiles to make it clear who owns them when they graze together in the desert.

DESERT EXPERTS

Wild Bactrian camels have two cone-shaped humps on their backs. The humps allow them to store fat, so they can survive without food for a long time. When they find a source of water, they will drink as much as 50 litres (88 pints). They will even drink salty water, unlike other mammals.

LOP NUR

In an area of the Gashun Gobi Desert in China lives the only remaining group of Bactrian camels that is not at risk from mixing with domestic camels. The Chinese government and the Wild Camel Protection Foundation are helping to protect an area known as the Lop Nur Nature Reserve. The hardy camels live and breed here, even though the site was a nuclear testing area for 45 years.

MEDICAL MARVELS

The one-humped camel, the dromedary, has been found to have an extraordinary immune system. This camel's milk has qualities that make it useful for treating human medical conditions, including diabetes.

PROTECTION WITHOUT BORDERS

Both the Chinese and Mongolian governments have agreed together to protect the wild Bactrian camel, because it lives on both sides of the border between the two countries.

A captive breeding programme also began in Mongolia in 2003. In 2013, as part of the programme, two captive-born wild bulls were successfully released into a protected natural habitat.

KEY FACTS

Scientific name: *Camelus ferus*
Size: Head and body length: up to 3.5m; tail length: 51–64cm; shoulder height: up to 1.8m
Diet: Leafy flowering plants and shrubs (woody stemmed plants)

Status: Critically endangered (population decreasing)
Amazing fact: Bactrian camels can survive in extreme cold and heat ranging from -40 to 55°C (-40 to 131°F).

SNOW LEOPARD

In the mountains of Central Asia lives the strikingly beautiful but increasingly rare snow leopard. The future of this remarkable big cat depends on experts from many countries agreeing on action plans – and carrying them out successfully.

Camera trap photo

SNOW WORRIES

With thick, woolly fur on its belly and long hair on its back, this hardy cat is protected from the harsh conditions where it lives. It is perfectly adapted to the habitat, and its diet keeps the numbers of smaller mammals under control. In turn, this protects the sparse plant-life of the mountains from being over-grazed.

PROTECTION PLANS

In Beijing, China, in 2008 a meeting was held to bring together experts from countries across the snow leopard's range. The aim was to share knowledge about the snow leopard and plan conservation efforts. Many of the countries now have action plans for how to help the leopard in their region.

They are known as ghosts of the mountains, and sometimes snow leopards' paw prints are the only clue to their location.

SNOWY SELFIE

To track snow leopard activity, wildlife biologists set up special cameras, hidden in piles of rocks. When the snow leopard passes near, it walks through a beam of infrared light. This triggers the camera to take a photograph, giving a vital glimpse of the cat in the wild.

BORDER BARRIERS

The worldwide snow leopard population is around 4,000–6,500. Their global range is patchy – including parts of 12 Asian countries. In many places their ranges cross country borders. Where there are wars between the neighbouring countries, it causes great risk to the leopards and any conservation efforts.

KEY FACTS

Scientific name: *Panthera uncia*
Size: Head and body length: up to 1.25m
Diet: Mainly mountain goats and sheep. In summer, it also easts marmots, pikas, rabbits, voles and pheasants.

Status: Endangered (population decreasing)
Amazing fact: The snow leopard's tail can be just over 1m long. It is used for balance on steep mountainsides and as a warming blanket, wrapped around its body when resting.

WRAP UP WARM

In Tibet, the wild yak are well adapted to life in the mountains. They have large lungs to cope with breathing the mountain air, which is low in oxygen, and powerful hearts to keep the blood pumping. Their fur has a matted undercoat and a shaggy outer layer, to keep as much body heat as possible.

WILD YAK

HELPFUL HERDS

Today there are around 12 million domestic yak. Traditionally, they were used for transport and to carry heavy loads. Today trucks are often used instead, but yaks still provide milk, butter, meat, fur and leather, and their dung is an important source of fuel.

For centuries, the nomadic people of the Tibetan Plateau have relied on herds of yak for survival. These domesticated animals are a different species to the larger wild yak, which now numbers just 10–15,000. To save it from extinction, the wild yak must be prevented from breeding with the domestic yak.

REMOTE REFUGE

The human population of the Tibetan Plateau has grown so much over the last 50 years that wild yaks have been pushed back to very remote areas. Now, nature reserves have been created and conservation charities work with domestic yak herders to protect the remaining wild yaks.

YAK FESTIVALS

The nomadic culture of Central Asia remains very strong, and the yak is a key part of their culture and lifestyle. Traditional yak festivals are held to honour the animal, with activities including yak polo, yak racing and yak rodeo as well as milking competitions.

KEY FACTS

Scientific name: *Bos mutus*
Size: Head and body length: up to 3.8m; tail length: up to 1m; shoulder height: up to 2m
Diet: Grasses and sedges (grass-like wetland plants)

Status: Vulnerable (population decreasing)
Amazing fact: Yaks can produce more milk than goats and sheep, but it goes off quickly. It is often made into butter, traditionally in a yak-skin bag.

BENGAL TIGER

Star of Indian folklore, the mighty, stripy tiger is an impressive and globally recognised predator. As the national animal of India and Bangladesh, this big cat symbolises strength and power, but like many other subspecies of tiger, the Bengal's rapidly falling numbers are now cause for great concern.

BENGAL BEAUTY

Found in India, Nepal, Bhutan and Bangladesh, the Bengal tiger, sometimes known as the Royal Bengal tiger, is the most numerous subspecies. It has a powerful, muscly body and can swim, climb and leap as far as 8–10 metres (26–33ft) in one bound. Females give birth to two to six cubs in a litter, and those that survive will stay with their mother until they are around two years old.

JOINED UP THINKING

The areas of forest that join up separate nature reserves, known as wildlife corridors, are vital pathways for tigers to mix and breed. In India, researchers have found that tigers will mate with others as far as 370km (230mi) away.

THE TIGER DANCE

The goddess Durga of the Hindu religion is often shown riding a tiger, and in the Indian state of Kerala, an annual harvest festival celebrates this big cat with people dressed up as tigers for the 'Pulikali' (meaning 'tiger dance').

PEOPLE POWER

In 2010, 13 countries that are home to tigers made an agreement to try to double tiger numbers by 2022. This involves tackling illegal poaching and trade, and carefully managing the natural habitat. Educating local people is also a key part of protecting the species.

← **Guards patrol nature reserves to deter poachers.**

TAG TEAMS

Tagging and monitoring tigers helps researchers learn about individuals in local areas. In India, a conservation programme called Project Tiger aims to protect the country's tiger population and its habitats. In China, nature reserves have been set up to protect the Amur tiger, which had been declared extinct there in 2007 but was rediscovered in 2015.

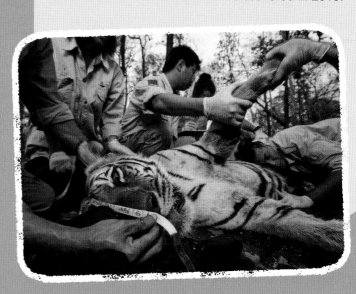

EXTINCTION IN OUR TIMES

Of the nine subspecies of tiger, three have already become extinct in the past 100 years. Over half the remaining tigers in the world are Bengal tigers. It is thought that tigers could become extinct in the wild within the next 10 to 12 years.

KEY FACTS

Scientific name: *Panthera tigris tigris*
Size: Head and body length: up to 2.9m; tail length: up to 1.1m
Diet: Mostly deer and pigs, occasionally animals as large as gaur (Indian bison)

Status: Endangered (population decreasing)
Amazing fact: There are now only around 2,300 Bengal tigers in Asia, living in small populations of less than 250 each.

This scorpion burrows into the ground during the day, then comes out at night to hunt.

MALAYSIAN FOREST SCORPION

Scorpions have walked the Earth for hundreds of millions of years. These hardy and adaptable creatures can survive on very little, and defend themselves with a powerful sting in the tail.

THE DEADLY FEW

There are around 2,000 different species of scorpion, but only about 30 have poison strong enough to threaten a person's life. The scorpions with the most dangerous stings include the Indian red scorpion, the deathstalker scorpion and the Arabian fat-tailed scorpion. The Malaysian forest scorpion has a painful, but not deadly sting.

Indian red scorpion

GLOW WILD

Scorpions have the surprising ability to glow a greenish blue colour under ultraviolet light. In the wild, the moonlight can cause this effect. By shining special lights around, scientists can easily spot them in the darkness. It is not yet fully understood why scorpions can do this.

SLOW PROCESS

One of the reasons Malaysian forest scorpions have survived on the planet so long is their remarkable ability to live on as little as one single insect per year. If food supplies run low, the scorpion can slow down its metabolism – the way the body processes energy from food – giving it much longer to find its next meal.

PRECIOUS VENOM

Medical scientists are testing the use of scorpion venom to find human brain cancer cells. Nicknamed 'tumour paint', the deathstalker scorpion's venom finds its way to cancer cells in the brain. Once found, these cells can be removed by a surgeon.

KEY FACTS

Scientific name: *Heterometrus spinifer*
Size: Length: up to 12cm
Diet: Mainly insects
Status: Not evaluated

Amazing fact: Unlike many invertebrates, the female forest scorpion gives birth to live young and carries them on her back until they moult (shed their skin) for the first time.

KING COBRA

The world's longest venomous snake is found in the forests of India and Southeast Asia. The king cobra feeds on other snakes, including its own species, and is highly venomous.

CLEVER KILLER

As its tongue flicks in and out of its mouth, the king cobra picks up scent particles from the air. It will also feel vibrations in the ground if prey is nearby. Once the cobra catches its prey and delivers the venom, it opens its flexible jaws wide and swallows the meal whole, head first.

DEFENCE DISPLAY

If threatened, a king cobra can raise its head up to a metre (3ft) off the ground. It also extends a hood around its neck, hissing to scare off the attacker.

RAINFOREST RESEARCH STATION

At the Agumbe Rainforest Research Station in Karnataka, southern India, the world's first radio-telemetry project on king cobras began in 2008. Radio transmitters were put inside the snakes, so they could be tracked and researchers could learn more about their movements and behaviour.

NEST EGGS

Female king cobras are the only snakes known to build a nest for their eggs. A mother will lay 20–50 eggs, then sit on top of the leafy nest to keep them warm. Then, just before they hatch around 90 days later, she leaves them to fend for themselves.

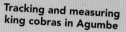

Tracking and measuring king cobras in Agumbe

KEY FACTS

Scientific name: *Ophiophagus hannah*
Size: Length: up to 5.5m, but rarely longer than 4.3m
Diet: Mainly other snakes
Status: Vulnerable (population decreasing)

Amazing fact: With this snake's excellent eyesight, it will notice prey moving as far as 100m away.

OCEANIA

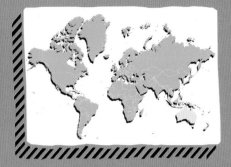

As its name suggests, Oceania is a region connected by the blue waters of the Pacific Ocean, rather than land borders. Located to the southeast of Asia, Oceania's largest countries are Australia, Papua New Guinea and New Zealand. Scattered across the region are many small volcanic and coral islands. Oceania feaures some of the world's most spectacular and largely untouched landscapes, including sandy beaches, tropical forests, snowy mountain ranges and Australia's rural outback.

PACIFIC PEOPLES

With a total population of around 40 million, Oceania includes large cities such as Sydney in Australia, with around five million people, as well as tiny islands where nobody lives at all. Native people include the Aboriginal Australians and the Maori of New Zealand.

Maori men performing a traditional war dance

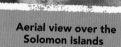

Aerial view over the Solomon Islands

ASIA

Indian Ocean

Papua New Guinea

Solomon Islands

Coral Sea

Vanuatu

Fiji

Pacific Ocean

New Caledonia (France)

Australia

SAFE HAVEN

Oceania is home to some unique wildlife, including many of the world's marsupials – mammals that mostly raise their young in pouches. Egg-laying mammals, such as the duck-billed platypus, are also found here. Movement of people and wildlife from other continents has brought new threats to the safe haven of Oceania.

ULURU

In the desert landscape of central Australia stands Uluru, also known as Ayers Rock. This large rock formation is sacred to the Aboriginal people and attracts hundreds of thousands of tourists each year.

Tasmania (Australia)

Tasman Sea

New Zealand

North Island brown kiwi with egg

RECORD BREAKERS

Of all the world's birds, kiwis lay the largest eggs in relation to their size. A female kiwi may lay an egg that weighs as much as a quarter of her weight. Sadly, many do not hatch, and without protection only five per cent of the chicks reach adulthood.

LITTLE SPOTTED KIWI

The little spotted kiwi is the smallest and most endangered of the five kiwi species. A national symbol of New Zealand, this surprising survivor was once considered extinct but has now become a conservation success story.

SHOCK OF THE NEW

Little spotted kiwis used to live on both the North and South Islands of New Zealand. Sadly, they died out on both islands, probably due to new predators arriving, brought by European settlers. Thanks to conservation efforts, little spotted kiwis now live in small populations on several islands, including Kapiti Island. Some have now been reintroduced to New Zealand's North Island.

ISLAND SANCTUARIES

Moving these flightless birds to islands where predators cannot threaten them has rescued little spotted kiwis from extinction. The population is now around 1,500, and considered stable and recovering, thanks to sanctuaries and community projects. To monitor kiwi numbers and locations, their calls are counted and specially trained dogs and radio tracking systems are used. In these safe habitats, more than half the kiwi chicks now survive.

Kiwis forage at night, in the leaf litter of the forest floor. Unlike any other bird, kiwis have nostrils at the end of their long beaks.

KEY FACTS

Scientific name: *Apteryx owenii*
Size: Length: up to 45cm
Diet: Mostly small invertebrates, especially earthworms, also beetle and cranefly larvae, caterpillars, spiders and the fruit of the hinau tree

Status: Near threatened (population stable)
Amazing fact: After the female little spotted kiwi has laid an egg, it is the male that will sit on the nest until it hatches. The hatchling will then stay close to him for about a month.

RED KANGAROO

This speedy hopper is the largest land mammal in Australia and the largest living marsupial in the world. Thriving in the grasslands of the Australia's rural outback, the red kangaroo has become a much-loved Australian icon, recognised all over the world.

LAND OF THE MARSUPIALS

The kangaroo is part of a group of mammals called marsupials, whose babies are born at a very early stage and complete their development feeding on their mother's milk, often inside a pouch. Most marsupials are native to Oceania, with a few found in the Americas. Red kangaroos are the largest of the marsupials, and can be told apart from other kangaroos by a light stripe on each side of the face, running from the chin up to each eye.

A newborn kangaroo attaches to a teat inside its mother's pouch.

SPEEDY SPRINGS

A male red kangaroo can leap up to an amazing 3m (10ft) into the air and cover a distance of up to 9m (30ft). This is achieved using powerful back legs, which act like giant springs allowing the kangaroo to bounce along at up to 64km (40mi) per hour.

RAISING ROOS

A female red kangaroo gives birth to one blind, hairless baby after only 33 days' development. The baby is very tiny, but climbs up into the mother's pouch where it attaches to a teat and feeds on milk. Once it is large enough, the young kangaroo, known as a joey, peeks out from inside the pouch to see the world. It won't leave the pouch permanently until around seven to eight months old, and may continue to suckle for longer.

Male red kangaroos can weigh as much as 92kg (203lbs), reaching double the body weight of the females.

AUSSIE ATTRACTION

There are many millions of red kangaroos in Australia and the national parks where they live are great tourist attractions. Kangaroos have partly benefitted from human settlements, which bring new watering holes and opportunities for food. However, humans bring risk too. Some kangaroos are hunted for leather and meat, but this is controlled by law. Many are injured by vehicles on Australia's highways, so rescue centres now care for injured adults and orphaned joeys.

A tourist holds a baby kangaroo in a specially made pouch at a rescue centre.

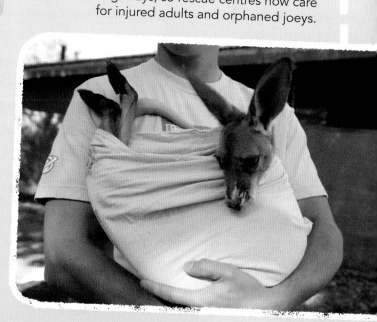

BOUNCING BOXERS

Kangaroos usually live in small groups, but in areas with a good food supply, they may gather in groups of over a thousand. Males, called 'boomers', will fight to win a female. Fighting fiercely, they use the power of their long back legs to kick each other, using their tail as a support. These fights can lead to broken bones, internal injuries and even the death of the weaker male.

KEY FACTS

Scientific name: *Osphranter rufus*
Size: Head and body length: up to 1.4m; tail length: up to 1m
Diet: Grasses and similar flowering plants, also leaves and fruits of certain shrubs
Status: Least concern (population stable)

Amazing fact: All at the same time, a mother kangaroo may have one baby feeding in its pouch, another that has left the pouch but returns to suckle, and a fertilised egg waiting to develop.

LEADBEATER'S POSSUM

There are many and various kinds of possum, but Leadbeater's possum in particular is one of the few creatures that have been declared extinct but survived to tell the tale. The remarkable story of this marsupial shows how important wildlife spotting can be in saving threatened creatures.

A researcher tattoos the ear of a Leadbeater's possum so it can be identified.

HOLLOW HOPES

Leadbeater's possum was not discovered until 1867 and is named after John Leadbeater, a naturalist at Museum Victoria in Australia. Also known as the fairy possum, it is very particular about its habitat. Living in colonies of between two to 12 possums, they need forest areas with trees of different ages, including old mountain ash trees for their nests. When forest is cut down, the trees may take 150 years to reach the right size for nesting.

SUGAR GLIDER

The sugar glider is a little possum widespread in Oceania and Indonesia. It glides among the trees, with 'wings' formed by a membrane stretching from its wrists to its ankles. The sugar glider's tail helps it to control the flight, and the sharp claws grip branches for a safe landing.

RISING FROM THE ASHES

Leadbetter's possum was thought to be extinct in 1960, as it had not been seen for 50 years, during which time terrible fires had destroyed much of its habitat. Then, in 1961, a young naturalist named Eric Wilkinson spotted a Leadbeater's possum in the forest. As an assistant at Museum Victoria, Eric quickly reported the exciting discovery. The species recovered well with special protection, but forest fires are still a great threat.

KEY FACTS

Scientific name: *Gymnobelideus leadbeateri*
Size: Head and body length: up to 17cm; tail length: up to 18cm
Diet: Wattle tree sap and honeydew, also insects and spiders

Status: Critically endangered (population decreasing)
Amazing fact: Feeding at night, around 80 per cent of this possum's diet is tree sap and honeydew, which it licks from leaves and branches. Honeydew is the sugary waste produced by some insects.

COMMON EMU

One of Australia's most famous animals, the emu is the second tallest bird in the world after the ostrich. Once hunted for meat and for the oil made from its fat, the emu became extinct in some areas, but it is now widespread and thriving in Australia.

DOWN TO DAD

Once a female emu has laid her eggs, the care is left to the male. He protects the nest fiercely, keeping the eggs warm and rotating them regularly until they hatch. This important job takes all his time and he will not eat until the young hatch. Then he protects the chicks and teaches them how to survive.

SIMILAR BUT DIFFERENT

The ratites are a group of flightless birds, the largest of which are the emu, ostrich and rhea. These larger ratites look similar, but they are found on different continents: the emu in Australia, the ostrich in Africa and the rhea in South America.

FENCED OFF

Emus help their environment by spreading seeds in their droppings over wide areas as they follow migration routes. However, because they feed on cereal crops, emus can cause problems for farmers. Fences are put up, some hundreds of kilometres long, to protect crops, but these can block emu migration routes and affect other wildlife.

FLIGHTS CANCELLED

Despite being a flightless bird, the emu can move at speeds of up to 50km (31mi) per hour – it runs. It has small wings that are described as vestigial, because they are no longer used for flying. Their shaggy brown feathers help to protect the emu from burning in the sunlight.

KEY FACTS

Scientific name: *Dromaius novaehollandiae*
Size: Length: 1.6m; height: up to 2m
Diet: Seeds, fruits and shoots of various plants, also insects and other small animals
Status: Least concern (population stable)

Amazing fact: If threatened, an emu can deliver a very powerful kick and its long talons can cause fatal injury to an attacker.

MERINO SHEEP

There are now more than a billion sheep worldwide, and in New Zealand they outnumber people six to one. Sheep have been an important source of meat and wool for thousands of years. Today many different breeds of sheep are farmed and a range of food and textile industries depends on them.

FLOCKING INSTINCT

For protection, sheep naturally gather and move together as a flock. This helps the sheep farmer, or shepherd, to control flocks as large as 1,000 sheep using specially trained dogs.

FLEECY FRIENDS

Sheep's fleece is sheared and spun to make wool, one of the most widely used animal fibres in the world. Woollen clothing and sheepskin are valued for their warmth and durability.

SUPERSTAR SHEEP

A Finnish Dorset sheep called Dolly became very famous in 1996. She was the first mammal to be successfully produced by a process called cloning, using the cell of an adult. Dolly had no father, and was an exact copy of her mother. Since then, a variety of cloning techniques have been used to clone many other kinds of animal.

NEW ZEALAND NEWCOMERS

Sheep were brought to New Zealand in the 1700s by British explorer Captain James Cook. During the 1800s, the flocks began to thrive and sheep farming became an important industry. The Merino breed was introduced later from Spain for its long, crimpy wool. By crossing Merino sheep with other breeds, farmers produced the Australian Merino, valued for both its meat and wool. There are now more than 75 million sheep in Australia.

KEY FACTS

Scientific name: *Ovis aries*
Size: Domestic breeds can vary greatly. Head and body length: 1.2–1.8m; shoulder height: 65cm–1.2m
Diet: Mainly native short grasses and similar flowering plants

Status: Domestic animal, not evaluated
Amazing fact: Wool is graded by the thickness of the fibres, measured in microns. Merino wool is usually under 24 microns and is valued for being very fine but also extremely strong.

GREY-HEADED FLYING FOX

Despite a fox-like appearance, this is not a fox at all but the largest bat in Australia. It lives in large colonies known as 'camps', numbering hundreds or even thousands. A diet of nectar, pollen and fruit makes flying foxes very important in their habitat for pollinating plants and trees as well as spreading seeds over large areas.

MICROBATS AND MEGABATS

Bats make up about a quarter of all mammal species. There are more than 90 species of bat in Australia, and around 1,300 worldwide, divided into two groups: microbats and megabats. The megabats, including flying foxes, are mainly fruit-eaters, while microbats feed mostly on insects and tend to be smaller.

PERFECT POLLINATORS

Grey-headed flying foxes will migrate to find their favourite plants in blossom, sometimes travelling as far as 50km (31mi). Their furry bodies carry pollen on the journey, often helping to pollinate plants over longer distances than birds and insects.

BAT RESCUE

Megabats face many human threats. Some are killed by power lines, while others are shot by farmers defending their crops. In response to large numbers of young flying foxes needing medical attention, a bat hospital has been created in Tolga, Australia. Here orphaned bats are hand-raised and hundreds are released back into the wild each year.

Researchers catch and test bats for signs of disease.

BAT ACTION PLAN

The Action Plan for Australian Bats was launched by the Australian government after bat numbers had dropped sharply. The plan triggered greater research into bat colonies and encouraged wildlife education.

KEY FACTS

Scientific name: *Pteropus poliocephalus*
Size: Head and body length: up to 29cm; wingspan: about 1m
Diet: Pollen, nectar and fruit
Status: Vulnerable (population decreasing)

Amazing fact: As well as drinking dew from leaves, flying foxes will 'belly dip' into rivers and lakes so that they can lick water droplets from their fur.

DUCK-BILLED PLATYPUS

One of the most curious of creatures, this egg-laying mammal has dense fur like an otter and a bill like a duck. When European scientists first studied duck-billed platypuses, preserved and shipped from Australia, they didn't believe they were real. Now this fascinating animal is protected as a national icon.

MARVELLOUS MONOTREMES

The duck-billed platypus is one of only five species of egg-laying mammals in a group known as monotremes. The group has two families, one containing the four species of echidna (spiny anteater) and the other containing only the platypus. It is the only living member of a family that existed 23 million years ago.

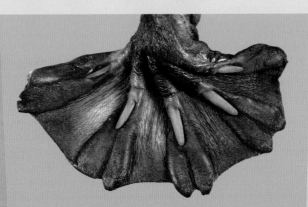

CURIOUS CLAWS

When swimming underwater, a platypus's front paws become powerful paddles. The digits of the front paws splay out and the webbing in between stretches into a fan shape. On land, this webbing folds back, exposing sharp claws for digging. Male platypuses have spurs on their hind legs that can deliver venom to an attacker or a rival male.

RIVER RECOVERY

Hunted for its fur in the past, the platypus is now protected by law and conservation programmes. The 'Wild Rivers' project has been established to protect waterways for threatened creatures. This project involves conservation groups, indigenous people and scientists. Together, they aim to control human activity and keep some areas of river untouched so that wildlife can thrive.

The platypus hides away in a burrow by the water's edge.

NOT SO HARD-NOSED

Despite its name, the duck-billed platypus does not have a hard bill like a bird. Instead, its bill is soft, leathery and very sensitive. Foraging at dusk and dawn, the platypus uses the bill to poke around in the soft mud of riverbeds, finding small freshwater creatures to eat.

HUNGRY HATCHLINGS

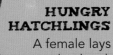

A female lays eggs that hatch after about ten days. She produces milk for her bean-sized hatchlings, which collects in grooves on her body so the babies can lap it up. Wildlife centres rescue orphaned platypuses and hand-rear them until they can survive in the wild.

KEY FACTS

Scientific name: *Ornithorhynchus anatinus*
Size: Length: up to 63cm
Diet: Mainly small invertebrates
Status: Near threatened (population decreasing)

Amazing fact: A platypus can hunt using sensors on its bill to detect electric signals given off by its prey. This helps it to hunt in the murky waters of the riverbed.

TASMANIAN DEVIL

The screeching night-time cries of this marsupial have earned it this impressive common name and its ability to crush the bones of its prey adds to its fearsome reputation. Found on the island of Tasmania, an island state of Australia, it is the largest meat-eating marsupial, feeding on any flesh it can find.

FIRST COME, FIRST SERVED

A female gives birth to as many as 15–20 young. Like other marsupials, the babies are not fully developed, and crawl to her pouch. Tasmanian devils' pouches are backwards-facing with only four teats, so only the babies that attach quickly will survive. Once they outgrow the pouch, the joeys ride on their mother's back until they can hunt for themselves.

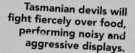

Tasmanian devils will fight fiercely over food, performing noisy and aggressive displays.

FACING EXTINCTION

The Tasmanian devil's range once included the Australian mainland, but it is now limited to Tasmania and nearby islands. In the last ten years, an infectious disease called devil facial tumour disease has killed more than half the population and is still spreading.

MEET THE DEVIL

A programme called Save the Tasmanian Devil has been set up to monitor healthy groups of devils, and scientists have discovered that some are developing resistance to the disease. The Tasmanian Devil Conservation Park in Taranna protects the species and attracts tourists to meet the famous marsupials.

KEY FACTS

Scientific name: *Sarcophilus harrisii*
Size: Head and body length: up to 65cm; tail length: up to 26cm
Diet: Kangaroos, wallabies, possums, wombats and carrion

Status: Endangered (population decreasing)
Amazing fact: Tasmanian devils can crunch through the bones and fur of their prey, so they make useful cleaners, removing all traces of dead animals.

KOALA

Often seen hugging the branch of a tree, the furry koala has become one of Australia's most popular tourist attractions. This much-loved marsupial is recognised all over the world, but its survival depends on the protection of Australia's eucalyptus forests.

THE LONG WAY DOWN

Koalas feed almost entirely on eucalyptus leaves, which gives them a smell like cough medicine. These leaves contain tannins that are toxic to most animals. The koala has a very long gut containing special bacteria that breaks down the tannins, so it can safely digest the leaves.

UP A GUM TREE

There are around 600 species of eucalyptus, also known as gum trees, but koalas will feed on only around 120 of them, and usually only two or three at any one location. They therefore need plenty of space to find enough food – usually around 100 trees for each koala. There are currently around 330,000 koalas in the wild, but damage to their habitat is causing this number to drop every year.

BRANCHING OUT

Koalas sleep in the trees for as much as 18 hours each day. Their long front limbs, sharp claws, and padded paws give them an excellent grip on the branches.

POUCH PROTECTION

The koala gives birth to a very tiny baby that completes its development in the safety of the pouch, where it feeds on milk for six to seven months. From around five to seven months old it also feeds on a substance called pap. This is a special kind of runny faeces (poo) that gives the joey the gut bacteria it will need to digest eucalyptus leaves when it leaves the pouch.

FIRE HAZARD

Bushfires can spread quickly in the Australian outback, and cause terrible damage. They can be started by natural causes such as lightning storms, or by human activity. Global warming increases the hot, dry conditions that often lead to bushfires and drought. Koalas are completely dependent on the trees, so they are at great risk when areas of eucalyptus forest are suddenly destroyed. As slow-moving creatures, many die in spreading fires known as firestorms.

A koala is given a drink of water by a firefighter after surviving a bushfire in Australia.

KOALA CROSSING

As the human population increases, koalas' natural habitat is being broken up and destroyed. Where new roads are built, koalas are at great risk from traffic. Hundreds of koalas are killed and many more injured every year by motor vehicles. Rescue organisations and hospitals have been set up to help injured koalas, and signs by the roadside now warn drivers where koalas may be likely to cross.

KEY FACTS

Scientific name: *Phascolarctos cinereus*
Size: Head and body length: up to 82cm
Diet: Mainly leaves from certain eucalyptus trees
Status: Vulnerable (population decreasing)

Amazing fact: Adult male koalas can make loud, low-pitched bellows that can be heard over long distances to communicate with others.

ANTARCTICA

The globe's most southerly point, the South Pole, is located on Antarctica. This continent is the driest, windiest and coldest place on Earth, with temperatures sinking to a bone-chilling -90°C (-130°F). It is an extreme habitat, home to only very well-adapted wildlife. No people live permanently here, but several thousand work in research centres, discovering the secrets of this frozen wilderness.

THE FROZEN DESERT

Nearly 90 per cent of the world's ice is in Antarctica and at its thickest point it measures 4.8km (3 mi). Some snow does fall, but rain is very rare, making Antarctica the world's largest desert.

Falkland Islands

South Atlantic Ocean

SOUTH AMERICA

Larsen C Ice Shelf

Weddell Sea

Ronne Ice Shelf

Amery Ice Shelf

ANTARCTICA

South Pole

Ross Ice Shelf

Shackleton Ice Shelf

Ross Sea

Southern Ocean

Indian Ocean

WORLD'S END

The tilt of the globe means the Antarctic winter brings months of continuous darkness when the South Pole is tilted away from the Sun. The summer then brings months of endless days without sunset. Most research and tourism happens in the summer, around the coasts.

EXTREME EXPLORATION

This unique continent plays a crucial role in sea levels and climate processes that affect the rest of the globe. Many countries have research stations on Antarctica. These include amazing buildings designed to cope with the extreme conditions.

The Halley VI Research Station

OCEANIA

CLEVER KILLERS

Orcas are powerful and intelligent hunters with a variety of hunting techniques. Some hunt in deadly pods (groups), working together to kill large whales or surround schools of fish. Several orcas will swim together to create waves large enough to knock prey off the ice and into the water. This is known as 'wave-washing'.

ORCA

One of the most widespread mammals after humans, the orca is found in most of the world's oceans, but is particularly common in Antarctic waters. Also known as the killer whale, it is the largest species of dolphin. Its fearsome common name comes from its ability to outsmart and overpower prey as large as seals and whales.

SEALIFE SECRETS

Worldwide, there are around 50,000 orcas, but exact numbers are unknown. There are several different groups of orca, so scientists think these may prove to be different species or subspecies.

Technology is helping marine researchers gather new information. Tags can be attached to orcas and tracked by satellite to record their journeys or measure the depths of their dives.

FAMILY FORTUNES

Some orcas stay in family groups for most of their lives. Pods of grandmothers, mothers and their young will travel together over many years, which allows each generation to learn hunting skills. They communicate with clicks, whistles and calls, and their body language includes leaping out of the water (breaching) and slapping the surface with their fins.

WATCH WITH CARE

People have a great interest in orcas, but these large and intelligent creatures are not suited to life in captivity. Instead, viewing them in the wild has become popular. Responsible wildlife-watching tours are organised by marine scientists to collect data and educate tourists.

KEY FACTS

Scientific name: *Orcinus orca*
Size: Length including tail: up to 9.8m
Diet: Marine mammals, turtles, seabirds, large fish
Status: Data deficient

Amazing fact: Orcas are long-living marine mammals, with some females reaching around 90 years old.

HOURGLASS DOLPHIN

This fast-swimming dolphin lives in the cold, deep waters of Antarctica. Its remote habitat means little is known about its behaviour, but more is being discovered. Sociable creatures, hourglass dolphins ride the waves in pods (groups) of around seven, with rare reports of pods as large as 100.

CLICK AND COLLECT

This dolphin is most often seen in the Antarctic Convergence, an area where the icy waters meet slightly warmer waters further north. It can be recognised by the white hourglass-shaped patches on its side. Like other dolphins, it finds its way and locates food by making clicks and listening for the echoes that bounce back from surrounding objects. This is known as echolocation.

RIDE THE WAVES

Hourglass dolphins often leap through the waves, creating an effect called a 'rooster tail' as the water sprays off their dorsal fins. Their remote habitat keeps them mostly protected from human activity, but global warming brings dangerous changes for a creature that relies on cool surface waters.

Commerson's dolphins (shown here) are a similar rare species, also found in the Antarctic.

BLIZZARD CONDITIONS

Surveys show there may be around 144,300 hourglass dolphins. Accurate numbers for both the hourglass and Commerson's dolphins are not yet known. Research in Antarctic conditions can be challenging, but marine biologists take every opportunity to study these rare creatures and gather vital data.

KEY FACTS

Scientific name: *Lagenorhynchus cruciger*
Size: Length including tail: up to 1.9m
Diet: Fish, squid and crustaceans
Status: Least concern (population unknown)

Amazing fact: Using echolocation, the hourglass dolphin makes particularly high-pitched clicks. These travel well through the open ocean, helping it to find prey at up to twice the distance of other dolphins.

BLACK-BROWED ALBATROSS

One of the world's largest seabirds, the black-browed albatross spends months at sea. When it is time to breed it comes to land, nesting by the coast in large colonies. In fishing areas, the birds follow vessels for food, but this dangerous habit can put them at great risk of injury.

Very long wings make this seabird an expert glider, capable of covering great distances.

PILLAR NESTS

Gathering on coastal slopes and cliff terraces, large colonies of black-browed albatrosses breed together. Pairs mate for life, and from around seven to 10 years old females will lay one large, white egg each year. Their pillar-shaped nests of mud, grass, seaweed and guano (poo) can be up to 50cm (20in) high. About 70 per cent of the population nest around the Falkland Islands, where they are protected and there are few predators.

COLOUR BY NUMBERS

Conservation projects include colour marking fledgling albatrosses with paint, so that they can be spotted easily. Their locations can then be recorded and compared. This is a very cost-effective way of monitoring large numbers of young birds.

BEWARE THE BYCATCH

Albatrosses follow fishing trawlers for their feeding opportunities but many are injured or killed by fishing equipment. Known as bycatch, this is a major threat to marine birds and mammals. It is thought that bycatch kills around 100,000 birds from the albatross family each year.

The greyish-white fluffy chicks hatch around December. By April or May the fledglings are ready to leave the nest.

KEY FACTS

Scientific name: *Thalassarche melanophris*
Size: Length: up to 96cm; wingspan: up to 2.4m
Diet: Mainly fish, krill and cephalopods (such as squid, cuttlefish and octopuses). They also eat marine invertebrates called salps, jellyfish and floating carrion.

Status: Near threatened (population decreasing)
Amazing fact: On Macquarie Island in the Pacific, introduced European rabbits have stripped grassland with their grazing, causing terrible damage to the nesting sites of albatross colonies.

EMPEROR PENGUIN

The largest of all living penguins, emperors huddle together on the Antarctic ice for survival and hunt in the icy waters. During the breeding season, males and females share family duties in one of the most extreme habitats on the planet. Perfectly adapted to a seemingly impossible environment, the emperor penguin is the icon of the Antarctic.

SHELTER FROM THE STORM

Emperors are perfectly adapted to life in Antarctica with their thick layer of fatty blubber, a covering of densely packed feathers, and clawed feet to grip the ice. They keep warm by huddling together in large groups. The huddle shifts constantly by tiny amounts, allowing penguins to make their way to the middle to warm up, and back to the edges to cool down.

DADS ON DUTY

Female emperor penguins lay a single egg, and immediately leave it behind as they set out to sea for up to two months to feed. During this time males look after the egg, balancing it on their feet, tucked into the special brood pouch. Here, the egg is warmed against the penguin's skin, surrounded by feathered flesh. By the time the mothers return, most chicks will have hatched. They feed on fish brought back up from their mothers' stomachs. The fathers then return to the sea. They have not fed at all during this time and may have lost as much as half of their body weight.

BREEDING IN THE BLIZZARDS

In March and April, at the start of the Antarctic winter, the emperors begin an amazing journey, marching over 100km (62mi) across the pack ice to their breeding grounds. They breed in blizzard conditions, when the freezing winds can reach 200km (124mi) per hour and temperatures can drop to -60°C (-76°F). By the time the chicks are ready to forage at sea for themselves, it will be the summer season, giving them the best chance of survival.

Aerial view of an emperor penguin colony on the Weddell Sea

Researchers record the weight of emperor penguins and attach satellite tags.

SEEN FROM SPACE

Emperor penguins were the first animal to have their entire species counted from space. Using aerial and satellite images, scientists have been able to count penguins more accurately than ever before. This has revealed a total population of around 595,000 – twice as many as previously thought. Emperor penguins are not classed as endangered, but the pack ice they rely on is disappearing. Scientists predict that by the year 2100, the emperor penguin population may have suffered a shocking drop of about one third of its current numbers.

ANTARCTIC PENGUINS
Only two of the world's penguin species breed on the Antarctic continent: the emperor and Adélie penguins. Many others live around the Antarctic and subantarctic islands, including the chinstraps, gentoos, rockhoppers, macaronis, king penguins and royal penguins.

KEY FACTS

Scientific name: *Aptenodytes forsteri*
Size: Height: up to 1.3m
Diet: Fish, squid and krill
Status: Near threatened (population stable)

Amazing fact: Emperors can stay under water for up to 27 minutes and dive as far as 500m deep.

The largest of all seals, the Southern elephant seal spends most of its time in the Antarctic waters, but comes to shore to moult and to breed. Its name describes the trunk-like nose and enormous size of the males, with the largest weighing up to an amazing 3.7 tonnes (4 tons).

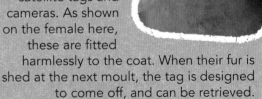

BATTLE OF THE BEACHMASTERS

Elephant seals spend most of the year foraging at sea to build up the blubber that keeps them warm and provides energy when they are on land. Males return first to the breeding grounds, but only the biggest and strongest will win the right to breed. When two large males compete, it can result in violent battles. The winners become 'beachmasters' and will breed with a group or harem of females.

Once on land in a harem, females do not feed, but rely on their blubber for nutrients while they give birth and suckle their pups.

PLAYING TAG

Technology allows researchers to track the movements and behaviour of elephant seals using satellite tags and cameras. As shown on the female here, these are fitted harmlessly to the coat. When their fur is shed at the next moult, the tag is designed to come off, and can be retrieved.

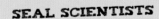

SEAL SCIENTISTS

Tracking tags have revealed that male and female elephant seals follow different migration routes in their search for food. As well as location, the tags record swimming speed, dive depths, and the temperature and salinity (saltiness) of the water. Gathering this important data also helps scientists to build up a picture of how the icy waters of Antarctica are changing over time.

KEY FACTS

Scientific name: *Mirounga leonina*
Size: Length: up to 5m (males are much larger than females)
Diet: Deep-water fish and squid
Status: Least concern (population stable)

Amazing fact: The Southern elephant seal is the deepest diver of all seals and walruses, swimming to depths of around 2km.

Many marine creatures depend on krill to eat, including penguins, fish, seabirds and even the mighty blue whale.

MARINE MEALS

Antarctic krill feed mostly on minuscule algae that gather on the sea ice. By eating the algae, and then being eaten themselves by larger creatures, krill play a vital role in passing energy up the food chain. Enormous swarms of krill move from the surface to deeper waters and back again, bringing a source of food to hundreds of creatures at different depths of the ocean.

ANTARCTIC KRILL

Krill are found in all the world's oceans, but without Antarctic krill most animal life in this harsh environment could not exist. Individually, Antarctic krill are no bigger than your finger, but together they form one of the most numerous species on Earth, supporting life not only in their own habitat but also in the wider world.

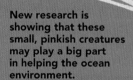

New research is showing that these small, pinkish creatures may play a big part in helping the ocean environment.

STRAIN ON THE FOOD CHAIN

Alarmingly, stocks of Antarctic krill have dropped dramatically in the last 40 years, possibly by as much as 80 per cent. There could be several reasons, but global warming is certainly a damaging factor. Scientists are busy researching the effect of climate change on this icy habitat. Any threat to krill puts an immediate and dangerous strain on the entire food chain.

Krill oil capsules

FISHING FOR PINK GOLD

In the Southern Ocean, fisheries harvest krill on an industrial scale, taking hundreds of thousands of tonnes each year. These krill are used in domestic animal feeds and their oil is used to make capules sold as health supplements. There is a global quota set to prevent overfishing, but many believe the Antarctic waters should be a zero-catch nature reserve.

Adélie penguins eat so much krill that their guano (poo) becomes pink and can stain their feathers.

KEY FACTS

Scientific name: *Euphausia superba*
Size: Length: up to 6.2cm
Diet: Mainly phytoplankton (microscopic marine plants), but in winter also zooplankton (tiny free-floating marine invertebrates), krill eggs and larvae, and detritus (fragments of waste)

Status: Least concern (population stable)
Amazing fact: Krill can live as long as 10 years – an incredible lifespan for creatures with so many predators.

OCEANS

Earth is known as the blue planet because vast areas of its surface are covered with water. Five ocean regions, known as the Arctic, Atlantic, Indian, Pacific and Southern oceans, together contain around 97 per cent of Earth's water. So far, we have discovered more than 230,000 species in the oceans. The ever-changing ocean waters are also key to our planet's water cycle, which is vital for humankind and all other life on Earth.

THE WORLD OCEAN

The five ocean regions combined are known as the World Ocean. Oceans and sea ice affect temperature and weather, playing an important role in how our planet works. When ice melts more of the sea's surface is exposed to the Sun and its temperature rises. Activities such as fishing, shipping and pollution also threaten ocean waters and put marine wildlife at risk.

Unmanned submersibles like China's Haidou-1 can dive to depths of more than 10,000m (6.2mi).

MYSTERIES OF THE DEEP

The Marianas Trench in the western Pacific Ocean is the deepest known part of the world's oceans. Underwater vessels called submersibles explore these depths, bringing samples and unknown species to the surface.

AGE OF DISCOVERY

Marine biologists think there may be as many as one to ten million species in the oceans. Science and technology are helping us to explore and find new species every year, making this a thrilling century of discovery.

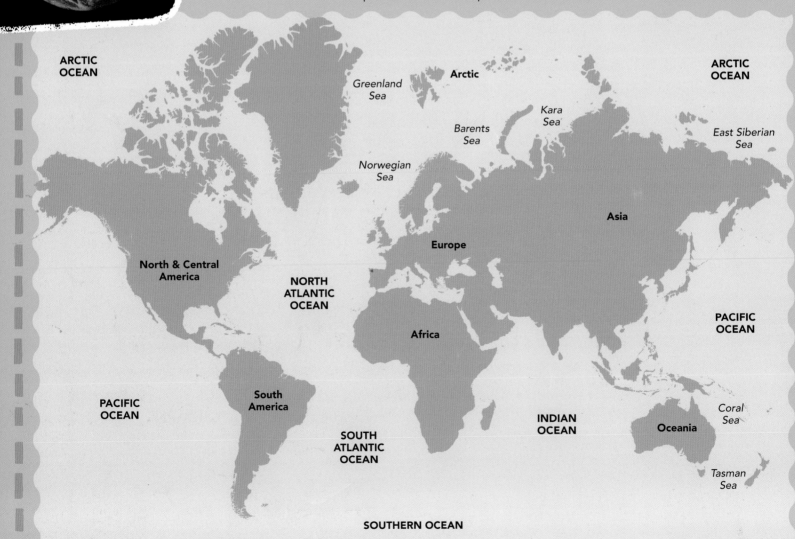

ARCTIC OCEAN

Arctic

Greenland Sea

Kara Sea

Barents Sea

East Siberian Sea

Norwegian Sea

ARCTIC OCEAN

Asia

Europe

North & Central America

NORTH ATLANTIC OCEAN

Africa

PACIFIC OCEAN

PACIFIC OCEAN

South America

INDIAN OCEAN

Oceania

Coral Sea

SOUTH ATLANTIC OCEAN

Tasman Sea

SOUTHERN OCEAN

LONG-SNOUTED SEAHORSE

This unusually shaped fish is part of a family that is unique to the animal kingdom: the males keep the eggs in a pouch and release the young when they hatch. The long-snouted or maned seahorse has a mane of fleshy spines running along the back of its neck, providing camouflage as it drifts among the rocks, seaweeds and seagrass in which it lives.

HUNDREDS BORN

A female long-snouted seahorse lays her eggs in a special brood pouch on the male's body. There, the eggs develop for three to five weeks before he pushes the live young out of his pouch. The young are tiny – measuring only 0.6–1.4cm (0.2–0.6in) – but as many as 500 may be released by just one male.

Baby seahorses emerging from the brood pouch of a male White's seahorse

SECRETIVE SEAHORSES

Found mostly in European waters, the population of long-snouted seahorses remains very mysterious, and it has been impossible to work out exact numbers. Some have been tagged and monitored (as shown here), but they may not represent the behaviour of the whole population. Seahorses have a limited ability to spread to new areas, so they can be very vulnerable to pollution or disturbance of their habitat.

Dried seahorses for sale in China

CAPTIVATING CREATURES

There are more than 40 different species of seahorse. Millions are harvested every year for a range of uses, which may pose a threat to the population. Their peaceful beauty makes seahorses very valuable to the aquarium trade and many are sold as tourist souvenirs. They are also used in traditional medicine, where they are linked with fertility and birth.

KEY FACTS

Scientific name: *Hippocampus guttulatus*
Size: Length: up to 21.5cm
Diet: Plankton
Status: Data deficient

Amazing fact: Unlike most fish, seahorses swim upright. Their dorsal fins beat at around 30–70 times per second to propel them through the water.

GREAT WHITE SHARK

This legendary fish is both admired and feared, and can be found in the coastal waters of all major oceans. Once believed to be a vicious man-eater, the great white is a purposeful predator with a range of sharp senses and a highly curious attitude.

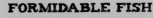

FORMIDABLE FISH

One of the largest predatory fish on Earth, the great white can weigh up to 2,268kg (5,000lbs). It can swim at 56km (35mi) per hour over short distances, and perform deadly attacks with not just one but multiple rows of blade-like triangular teeth. With a sharp sense of smell and the ability to sense even tiny movements in the water, the great white can track prey with great accuracy. Its incredible sensitivity can pick up electric signals as tiny as half a billionth of a volt, so even if prey is completely still, a passing great white will notice a heartbeat.

HUMAN VERSUS SHARK

Since the bestselling book and movie *Jaws* showed the great white to be a dangerous killer, people's fear of sharks has overshadowed their limited threat. In fact, humans are a far greater threat to the great white. Human development in coastal waters affects their breeding and feeding grounds, and many are still harmed by illegal hunting and fishing activity.

KEY FACTS

Scientific name: *Carcharadon carcharias*
Size: Length including tail: up to 6m
Diet: Various sea creatures, from large marine mammals to small fish
Status: Vulnerable (population unknown)

Amazing fact: Great white sharks can live as long as 70 years, much longer than the 23 years previously estimated.

THE BIG THREE

Bull sharks, tiger sharks and great whites are known as the 'Big Three' and are responsible for more than half of all shark attacks on humans. However, a closer look at the figures shows their deadly reputation is greatly exaggerated. More people are using the oceans than ever before, but fewer than two a year are killed by these sharks. They prefer a fatty meal, such as a seal or other marine mammal. Humans are more likely to be struck by lightning than attacked by a shark.

Attaching tags to great white sharks allows researchers to track their movements.

Near South Africa, sharks can charge up through the deep water, breaching the surface to grab prey.

TRANSFORMING TOURISM

The popularity of shark souvenirs and curios, such as teeth and fins, made them very valuable to hunters. Today, many people prefer to see sharks alive in marine aquariums and in the wild, so responsible tourism is helping to protect the species. Tours run by marine biologists and shark experts raise money for research and provide a way for people to learn about these fascinating predators in their natural environment.

KEEP IT REAL

Protecting the future of the great white depends on learning more about its true behaviour and encouraging people to respect this impressive hunter. The Australian government's White Shark Recovery Plan aims to limit the threats we cause, and is regularly updated based on new information discovered by marine scientists.

STAGHORN CORAL

Coral may look more like a rocky structure than a living thing, but it is made up of many tiny creatures called polyps. Some corals live as just one polyp, others form a single colony and some colonies create large reefs. Despite their small size, the combined power of many polyps provides an environment ideal for a huge variety of sea life.

ALGAE ADVANTAGES

Staghorns are among the fastest growing corals. The driving force of a coral reef is the special relationship between the coral and the algae that grows inside them. The coral provide the algae with the right environment to live, while the algae make nutrients from sunlight, feeding the coral it grows upon. This careful balance is vital to the success of the reef.

CORAL CATASTROPHE

Coral is harvested for use in jewellery and aquarium products, and is also threatened by human pollution. Many of the world's reef-building corals could face extinction due to global warming and an effect known as 'coral bleaching'. Warmer waters can put coral under stress, causing it to expel its algae, turn white and eventually die.

Coral conservation organisations transplant coral to damaged areas to encourage regrowth.

THE GREAT BARRIER REEF

The world's largest coral reef system is in the Coral Sea off the coast of Australia. Large enough to be seen from space, the Great Barrier Reef extends over an area of around 344,400 square kilometres (133,000sq mi) and contains around 2,900 reefs and 900 islands. This incredible place attracts many hundreds of different species of wildlife, as well as more than two million human visitors each year.

KEY FACTS

Scientific name: Acropora cervicornis
Size: The fast-growing branches can enlarge by up to 20cm each year
Diet: Plankton. The algae that live in their tissues also give them nutrients.

Status: Critically endangered (population stable)
Amazing fact: In 2005, around half the coral reefs of the Caribbean were lost in one year because of a massive coral bleaching event caused by warming ocean temperatures.

COMMON STARFISH

This five-armed starfish, found in a range of orange, brown and red shades, is the most common starfish in the north-east Atlantic. Despite having no jaws or teeth, the common starfish is a very successful predator, feeding on a range of marine life. With the ability to re-grow lost limbs and produce vast numbers of offspring, starfish are remarkably hardy creatures.

This starfish is turned upside down to show how its stomach slides out of its mouth.

STOMACH-TURNING TECHNIQUE

A starfish has many tube feet, armed at their tips with suckers to prise open the shells of bivalves such as mussels. It then inserts parts of its own stomach into a gap of just 0.1mm (0.004in). Wrapping its stomach around the soft parts of its prey, the starfish begins to break down its meal with digestive juices. It then gathers its stomach back into its own body to finish its meal.

MULTIPLY IN MILLIONS

A female starfish releases around 2.5 million eggs into the sea. The eggs and larval stages are eaten by many sea creatures. Adults are tougher, with fewer predators and the amazing skill of regenerating – or growing back – up to four of their arms. They can also reproduce simply by splitting. These remarkable abilities are being explored for use in human medicine.

Starfish larva (magnified)

CROWN-OF-THORNS STARFISH

At the Great Barrier Reef, crown-of-thorns starfish have caused so much damage by feeding on coral that a starfish-targeting robot has been created. Known as COTsbot, it helps to control the large numbers of starfish by injecting them with poison. The high population may be caused by over-fishing natural predators, or by warmer waters encouraging breeding.

KEY FACTS

Scientific name: *Asterias rubens*
Size: Diameter: up to 15cm
Diet: Molluscs, worms and other echinoderms, also carrion
Status: Not assessed

Amazing fact: If a starfish is split into five pieces, so long as each piece contains part of the central disc, then five starfish will survive.

SPERM WHALE

The sperm whale is an awe-inspiring marine mammal made famous in its role as the legendary white whale in the classic novel *Moby Dick*. Found in all but the coldest ocean waters, the sperm whale population was over a million until whaling ships brought numbers down to just a few hundred thousand. Human treatment of the whale has now greatly improved, but this ocean giant remains at risk.

Whales' teeth were made into decorative objects called scrimshaw.

CURIOUS USES

Historically, sperm whales were killed in shocking numbers for substances in their bodies called ambergris and spermaceti oil. These were used in many products including cosmetics, lamps and candles. Today, sperm whale hunting has largely stopped. Around the world, 88 countries are members of the International Whaling Commission, which manages the conservation of whales and the whaling industry.

GIANT STATISTICS

The gigantic box-like head of the sperm whale takes up around a third of its length, making it very easily recognisable. It can grow to an impressive weight of 45 tonnes (50 tons) and is the deepest diving mammal, plunging to depths of around 3km (2mi) in search of prey.

A sperm whale's blowhole is its left nostril, while the right one is used to make sounds.

When sperm whales come up for air, they blow about 20–70 times before diving again.

AIDING RECOVERY

The recovery of the sperm whale population takes time, particularly as female sperm whales produce just one calf every three to six years. Whales are still at risk from boat traffic, fishing equipment and pollution. Conservation workers and volunteers play a vital role, rescuing injured or beached whales.

A beached sperm whale is successfully returned to the ocean in Japan.

KEY FACTS

Scientific name: *Physeter macrocephalus*
Size: Length including tail: up to 19.2m
Diet: Mainly cephalopods (octopuses, squid, cuttlefish and nautiluses)
Status: Vulnerable (population unknown)

Amazing fact: The sperm whale has the largest and heaviest brain on Earth, weighing around 9kg.

HELPING HORSESHOES

Startling in its baby-blue colour, the copper-based blood of the horseshoe crab has a special clotting quality. It has become very valuable in testing the safety of human vaccines and medical equipment, and is said to be worth $15,000 a litre. Each year, around half a million crabs are bled and released, but some do not survive.

ATLANTIC HORSESHOE CRAB

Found along the east coast of North America, the horseshoe crab is part of a family that has thrived on Earth for hundreds of millions of years, since long before the dinosaurs. Now, demand for their special blue blood has begun to threaten this otherwise hardy creature.

LIVING MUSEUMS

When it is time to breed, large numbers of horseshoe crabs gather in shallow water by the coast. Their eggs are an important source of food for seabirds, turtles and fish. Many other marine creatures such as algae, barnacles and molluscs are found living on the large shells of horseshoe crabs, giving them the nickname 'living museums'.

CRAB CAMS

Horseshoe crabs are fitted with tracking tags and cameras for research. Scientists are studying the effects of blood collection to protect this useful species.

Full of surprises, the horseshoe crab has a total of nine eyes and a sword-shaped tail containing light-sensing organs.

KEY FACTS

Scientific name: *Limulus polyphemus*
Size: Length including tail: up to 60cm
Diet: Marine worms, molluscs and algae
Status: Vulnerable (population decreasing)
Amazing fact: Horseshoe crabs are not true crabs, but more closely related to the arachnid family, which includes spiders and scorpions.

LION'S MANE JELLYFISH

Jellyfish are curious creatures with no bones, no blood, no heart and no brain! More accurately known as sea jellies, they are not fish but soft-bodied marine creatures that have existed on Earth for at least 500 million years. The lion's mane jellyfish, found in the Atlantic Ocean, is the largest of them all.

The lion's mane jellyfish is bioluminescent, meaning it can glow in dark waters.

STEER CLEAR

The lion's mane jellyfish earned its name from its colours. It is 95 per cent water, but its stunning size and pulsing swimming action make it one of the most amazing creatures to watch. Each of its tentacles holds hundreds or even thousands of stinging cells. Even a dead lion's mane jellyfish or torn tentacles can deliver a nasty sting.

SEA SWARMS

This successful species moves readily to find food and can cover long distances helped by ocean currents. Jellyfish larvae attach to rocks, where they become polyps. Buds produced by the polyps grow into adult jellyfish. If conditions are right, jellyfish can form very large groups called swarms.

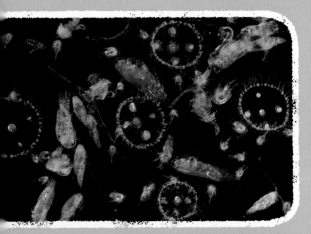

THE POWER OF PLANKTON

Zooplankton, shown magnified here, includes many extremely tiny organisms (microorganisms) and the larval stages of many sea creatures. Jellyfish are a type of zooplankton, but they can grow to be much larger than most plankton. Floating freely in the oceans, zooplankton is eaten by many sea creatures and forms a vital part of the food chain.

KEY FACTS

Scientific name: *Cyanea capillata*
Size: Length: up to 60m; diameter: up to 2m
Diet: Plankton, small fish and other jellyfish
Status: Not evaluated

Amazing fact: The largest lion's mane jellyfish ever found was longer than a blue whale, putting this species among the longest animals on Earth.

TEXTILE CONE

Also known as the cloth-of-gold cone, this sea snail has an attractive glossy patterned shell, but can be deadly. Found in sandy lagoons and coral reefs, it hides easily but can deliver a powerful venomous sting, lethal to its prey and even occasionally fatal to humans.

This image from a special kind of microscope shows the sharp tip of a cone shell's venom harpoon.

STEALTHY SHELL

Shaped like an ice-cream cone, the textile cone has eye stalks at its narrow end as well as a special tube used to smell food and breathe even while it is hidden beneath the sand. Once prey is found, the textile cone shoots out a long harpoon-like weapon that can deliver enough venom to paralyse the meal.

MARVELLOUS MEDICINE

Cone shell venom contains hundreds of different toxins and varies between species. It is thought to have killed around 30 people, and there is no antivenom. Despite the danger, cone shells may offer many possibilities for human medicine. The venom has very strong pain-relieving qualities. By studying the different kinds of cone shell, scientists hope to discover more about the natural power of their sting.

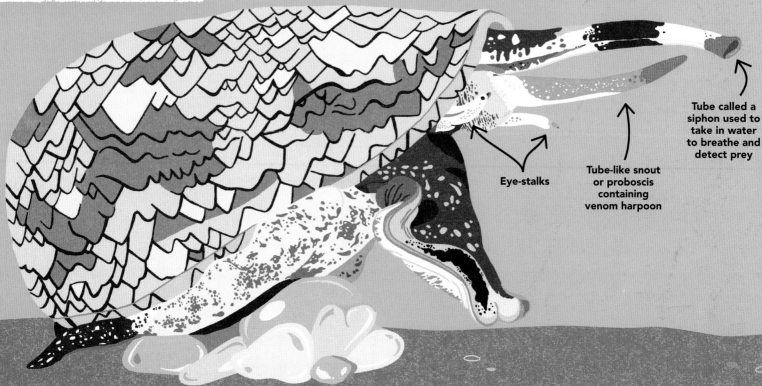

Eye-stalks

Tube-like snout or proboscis containing venom harpoon

Tube called a siphon used to take in water to breathe and detect prey

KEY FACTS

Scientific name: *Conus textile*
Size: Length: up to 15cm
Diet: Other sea snails, worms, small fish and some types of carrion
Status: Least concern (population unknown)

Amazing fact: The danger of the cone shells' venom is little-known, so many injuries are caused by people picking up the attractive shells on beaches or when diving.

SEA OTTER

One of the smallest marine mammals, the sea otter was hunted to the edge of extinction for its beautiful, thick fur. It became so rare that it took international agreement to save the population. The sea otters' recovery is an important success for ocean conservation and there are now more than 100,000 worldwide.

CRUCIAL COATS

Otters do not have blubber like other sea mammals and rely instead on their thick, shiny fur for survival. They have the densest fur of any mammal: a large male has around 800 million hairs, compared to just five million on a human. To keep their coats waterproof, otters spend a great deal of time grooming. They also blow air into their dense underfur, forming a layer of insulation that helps them stay warm even in cooler waters.

PUP PROTECTION

Sea otters use long strands of kelp, a seaweed, as anchor points. Wrapping themselves in the kelp, otters can rest or sleep without drifting away. Young, known as pups, cannot dive until they are two months old, and remain dependent on their mothers for around eight months. They are wrapped securely in kelp while the mother feeds.

TOOLS OF THE TRADE

Perfectly adapted to its aquatic lifestyle, the sea otter dives to the seabed to find mussels, snails, crabs and urchins, storing them in built-in pockets under its arms. At the surface, the otter rests on its back, using its chest as a table. For particularly hard shells, otters use rocks as tools to get to the soft meal inside. To feed on abalone shells, which stick to the rocks with great force, otters will strike them over and over, diving down several times to free their prize.

KEY FACTS

Scientific name: *Enhydra lutris*
Size: Head and body length: up to 1.2m; tail length: 25–37cm
Diet: Mainly marine invertebrates, including abalone, sea urchins, crabs and other molluscs

Status: Endangered (trend decreasing)
Amazing fact: A sea otter's tooth enamel is more than twice as strong as that surrounding human teeth, and can bite through a sea urchin's spines.

KEEPERS OF THE KELP

Sea otters keep the numbers of sea urchins under control, allowing kelp forests to thrive. As a keystone species, the daily lives of the otters balance the habitat around them, providing a safe home for many other creatures. The oil spill from the Exxon Valdez tanker in Alaska in 1989 killed several thousand sea otters because of the devastating effect of oil on their fur. Marine wildlife organisations now respond very quickly to oil spills with rescue and clean-up operations, but there is always lasting damage.

Researchers catch sea otters near Alaska to monitor the effects of the local oil spill.

CLOWN ANEMONEFISH

This eye-catching fish lives in the warm waters of the Indian and Pacific Oceans, in a particularly unusual home. Found among the stinging tentacles of sea anemones, it depends on a special covering of protective mucus. The appeal of this beautiful fish has led to a huge increase in demand from the aquarium trade.

BABY BOYS

Amazingly, all clown anemonefish are born male, with the ability to become female. They live in small groups, in which only the largest male and female breed. If the female dies, the largest male will become female, and one of the other males takes his role as the breeding male. Eggs are laid in large batches of 100–1,000. Successful breeding depends on water temperature, so global warming is a threat to the species.

A HAPPY HOME

The relationship between the fish and the anemone in which it lives benefits both creatures. The anemone provides a home and protection for the fish, while the fish removes parasites and circulates water around the anemone's tentacles.

AQUARIUM AWARENESS

This bright orange jewel of a fish was one of the first marine aquarium species to be bred successfully in captivity. The Disney Pixar movie *Finding Nemo* in 2003 led to a boom in demand for clown anemonefish in the pet trade. Marine biologists encourage people to check the source of their aquarium fish to protect the world's reefs and prevent any species being over-fished in the wild.

KEY FACTS

Scientific name: *Amphiprion ocellaris*
Size: Length: up to 11cm
Diet: Zooplankton, algae and parasites, found among the tentacles of the sea anemone
Status: Not evaluated

Amazing fact: The clown anemonefish will defend their anemone against other small fish that may want to eat it, but they themselves will eat any dead tentacles, helping to keep the anemone clean.

RED LIONFISH

Like a red and white firework, the lionfish's appearance is an explosive display. From a family of fish known as scorpionfish, they defend themselves with powerful venom. Native to the tropical waters of the South Pacific and Indian Oceans, lionfish also now thrive as an invasive species in the Caribbean and western Atlantic.

STEER CLEAR OF SPINES

The red lionfish can deliver venom through some of its sharp spines. This is used in defence against predators, but can also cause a painful wound to a human. Scorpionfish (the family it belongs to) are responsible for around 40,000–50,000 stings each year, second only to stingrays.

X-ray of red lionfish, showing needle-like spines

The striped pattern of the lionfish may seem easy to spot, but against a coral reef it provides the perfect camouflage.

Licensed divers catch lionfish in collection tubes.

INVASION OF THE LIONS

The cause of the lionfish's arrival in the western Atlantic is not known. It is thought that some aquarium owners may have released pet fish back to the wild when they became too big or aggressive. It is also possible that lionfish larvae were spread in the large water tanks of ocean vessels. With no natural predators in the area, lionfish breed rapidly and become a threat to local species.

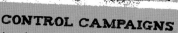

CONTROL CAMPAIGNS

Despite the risk of a sting, lionfish make popular sightings for reef divers. The U.S.A.'s National Oceanic and Atmospheric Association (NOAA) encourages lionfish awareness and educates divers on how to report sightings. They have also launched an 'Eat Lionfish' campaign to encourage people to enjoy lionfish dishes to help control numbers.

KEY FACTS

Scientific name: *Pterois volitans*
Size: Length: up to 38cm
Diet: Small fish, shrimps and crabs
Status: Not evaluated

Amazing fact: From just one year old, a female lionfish can produce thousands of eggs every four days, and up to two million eggs a year.

COMMON OCTOPUS

This master of disguise is thought to be the most intelligent invertebrate. It is highly curious and capable of using tools and learning from its behaviour. Scientists believe that by studying the very different intelligence of the octopus, we are likely to learn more about how our own brains work.

HIDDEN HUNTER

Found in temperate and tropical waters throughout the world, including the Mediterranean and the eastern Atlantic, the common octopus should be easy to recognise with its large head and eight arms covered with two rows of suckers. However, it can change colour according to its mood or to match its environment. It can also squeeze into impossibly tiny spaces, so predators and even divers often swim past without spotting it.

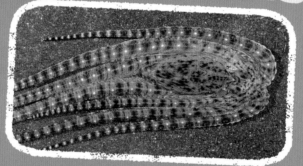

A mimic octopus pretending to be a flatfish

QUICK CHANGE

Like the common octopus, the Indonesian mimic octopus changes its skin colour and texture to blend with rocks and coral. But the mimic has an extra trick – it can also copy the shape and behaviour of a range of different creatures, including a flatfish, a lionfish or even a waving group of sea snakes.

The common octopus can change its appearance to blend in with the the colour, pattern and texture of its surroundings.

KEY FACTS

Scientific name: *Octopus vulgaris*
Size: Length: up to 1.3m
Diet: Crustaceans, especially crabs, and molluscs
Status: Not evaluated
Amazing fact: As well as the brain in its head, this clever creature also has packets of nerve cells in each of its arms, like a network of smaller brains.

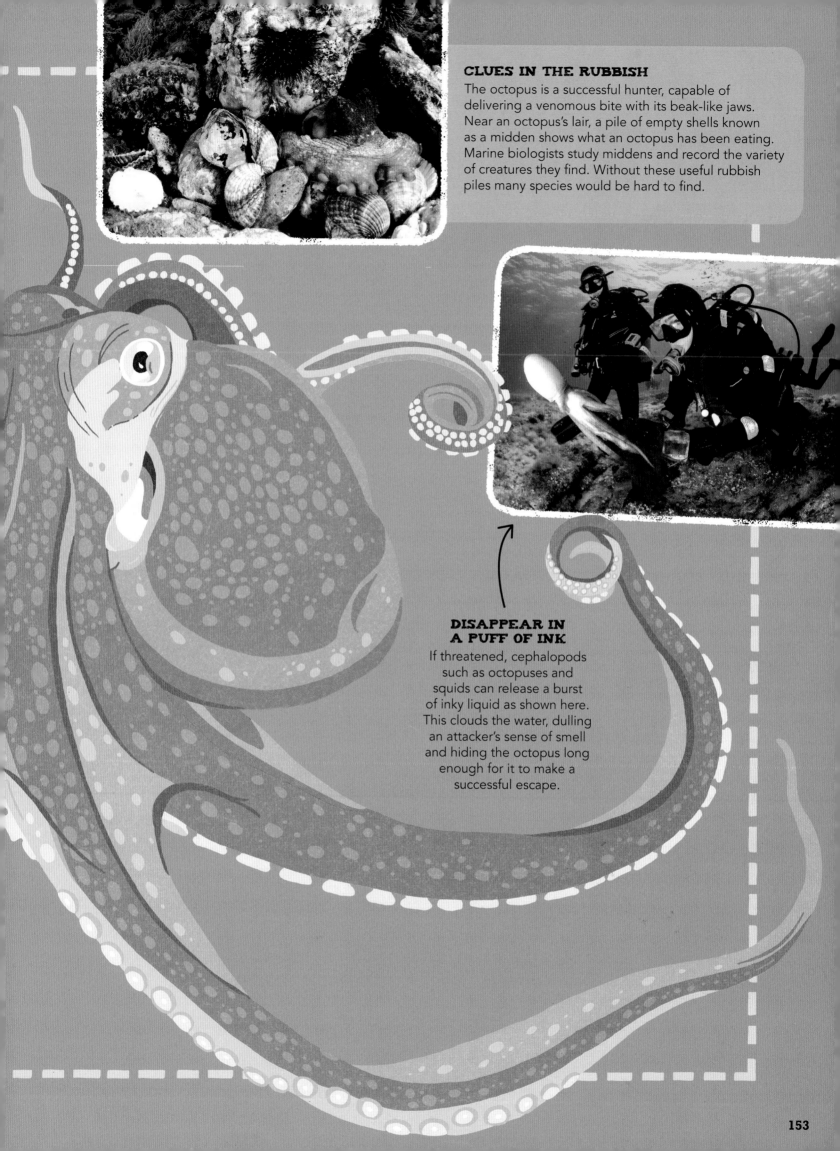

CLUES IN THE RUBBISH

The octopus is a successful hunter, capable of delivering a venomous bite with its beak-like jaws. Near an octopus's lair, a pile of empty shells known as a midden shows what an octopus has been eating. Marine biologists study middens and record the variety of creatures they find. Without these useful rubbish piles many species would be hard to find.

DISAPPEAR IN A PUFF OF INK

If threatened, cephalopods such as octopuses and squids can release a burst of inky liquid as shown here. This clouds the water, dulling an attacker's sense of smell and hiding the octopus long enough for it to make a successful escape.

LEATHERBACK TURTLE

The largest living turtle, the leatherback, is found in all the world's oceans. It has a flexible shell covered with strong, rubbery skin with a leathery appearance. Males spend their lives at sea, but females come ashore to lay eggs. The dangerous journey of the hatchlings from their nests to the ocean attracts great human interest.

BEACH BABIES
A female leatherback will usually return to the same region to nest, though not always the same beach. Nesting at night, she buries her eggs in the sand. After around 65 days the hatchlings emerge. Males hatch from eggs in cooler parts of the nest, while females develop in warmer areas.

PERILS OF PLASTIC
It is surprising that these large, active creatures live almost entirely on jellyfish, which are mostly water. Lion's mane jellyfish are a favourite food, and leatherbacks will swallow many with ease despite the stinging tentacles. Sadly, this prey is easily confused with plastic bags floating in the oceans, which cause injury and death to many sea turtles.

Green sea turtle

HERE COME THE GIRLS
Climate change is likely to have a terrible effect on sea turtles, who are long-living and slow to adapt. Warmer temperatures at nesting sites lead to more females hatching than males, which threatens the success of future breeding seasons.

EGGS OFF THE MENU
In Southeast Asia, turtle eggs are eaten as a delicacy. Breeding beaches are now being protected as well as the turtles themselves. Eggs in threatened areas are collected and moved to a hatchery, as shown above. Later, the hatchlings will be safely released.

KEY FACTS

Scientific name: *Dermochelys coriacea*
Size: Total length (beak tip to tail tip): up to 3.05m
Diet: Mainly jellyfish
Status: Vulnerable (population decreasing)

Amazing fact: Only about one in every 1,000 leatherback hatchlings will survive to adulthood, which takes 20–30 years.

LONG-SPINED PORCUPINEFISH

Found in tropical waters, this fish is also known as the balloonfish. If threatened, a porcupinefish will quickly show how unpleasant it would be as a meal, swelling to two or three times its usual size, making its long spines stick out all over.

SUPER STRETCH

This unusual fish can expand rapidly by sucking in water or air. Whether a marine creature attacks under water, or a seabird or human collector snatches it from above, a porcupinefish shocks its attacker with a spiky display. It has no scales, but stretchy skin and an elastic stomach for the balloon effect.

An uninflated porcupinefish has a flatter shape.

FANCY SOME FUGU?

Closely related to the porcupinefish (Didontidae) are the pufferfish (Tetraodontidae), which contain a toxic chemical that makes them very dangerous to eat. Some porcupinefish also have small amounts of this toxin. In Japan and Korea, the meat of the poisonous pufferfish is eaten as a delicacy, carefully prepared by licensed chefs. Known as fugu, this risky meal still causes accidental poisonings and even some deaths.

SHELLFISH SUPPER

With its solid, beak-like mouth, a porcupinefish can easily crack open the shells of hermit crabs, sea urchins and snails. It feeds at night, using its tail to steer and explore coastal areas and coral reefs to find hidden prey. Large eyes allow it to hunt at night, and although it cannot swim very fast, the porcupinefish is a successful hunter.

KEY FACTS

Scientific name: *Diodon holocanthus*
Size: Total length: up to 50cm
Diet: Molluscs, sea urchins, crabs
Status: Least concern (population unknown)

Amazing fact: Not all predators avoid porcupinefish. Tiger sharks will swallow them, spines and all, and seem unaffected by their toxins.

GIANT SQUID

This mysterious and magnificent marine creature is the longest known squid. The giant squid and its close relation the colossal squid, which is heavier, are the largest molluscs on Earth. Despite its incredible size, the giant squid is one of the most mysterious creatures of the oceans. Recent technology is allowing us glimpses of its fascinating life in the very darkest depths.

A giant squid beak, found in the gut of a sperm whale

READY FOR A CLOSE-UP

In 2004, researchers from the National Science Museum of Japan took the first photographs of a live giant squid in its natural habitat. They lured their target with a baited line attached to a remote underwater camera. Two years later, in 2006, they also succeeded in filming and capturing a giant squid for further research.

SUCKERED UP

With eight arms and two long feeding tentacles, the giant squid makes a fearsome predator. Prey is captured using saw-like sucker rings called tentacle clubs on the end of the feeding tentacles. Then the meal is hauled in to the squid's sharp, muscular beak, where it is shredded and swallowed.

SMART AND STEALTHY

Working out exactly where the secretive giant squid lives is a challenge, but they are known to exist in the North Atlantic, the North Pacific, and near the coasts of South Africa and New Zealand. Very few have been found, but their complex nervous system and very large brain are of great interest to scientists.

MEET THE FAMILY

Whenever new specimens are discovered, they reveal fascinating details about the life of this shadowy creature. Very little is known about their breeding habits, but a female was found with over 5kg (11lbs) of eggs inside – more than a million in total.

Marine biologists examining a giant squid

KEY FACTS

Scientific name: *Architeuthis dux*
Size: Total length: estimated up to 13m, possibly even longer
Diet: Small fish, crustaceans, other cephalopods
Status: Least concern (population unknown)

Amazing fact: The giant squid and the colossal squid have the largest eyes on Earth. At around 25cm across, they help squid see even in the dark depths of the ocean.

SILVER-LIPPED PEARL OYSTER

This remarkable creature is the largest of the pearl oysters – molluscs with the incredible ability to produce a beautiful pearl inside their shells. The high demand for these oysters' shells and their pearls has given rise to a worldwide industry, and those that make the most perfect pearls are highly prized.

Oysters hanging in nets at a cultured pearl farm

PRODUCING A PEARL

Oysters feed by filtering food from the water. If a hard particle enters the shell by accident, the oyster reacts by covering the item with layers of shell material called nacre, which builds up over several years to form a pearl. Pearls only occur naturally in about one in 10,000 oysters. In a process called 'culturing', oysters are collected from the wild and particles are inserted to grow into cultured pearls.

Oyster shell, known as 'mother-of-pearl', is used to make jewellery and buttons. The highly valuable gems of the silver-lipped pearl oyster are known as South Sea pearls.

BOY, GIRL, BOY, GIRL

Oyster larvae float through the open waters of the oceans as plankton. Many are eaten by other creatures, but some survive to attach themselves to a rock at the sea floor by little threads. Once attached, a pearl oyster may live as long as 40 years. At around three to four years old, all oysters are males. Then, when they reach a particular size, they all change to female. As they grow, they can switch sexes, but the overall balance of the population is maintained.

NATURE'S WATER FILTER

As filter-feeders, oysters play an important cleaning role. Capable of filtering huge volumes of water, they help to maintain the natural chemical balance of the oceans. Heavily polluted waters can upset this balance, proving too much for the oysters' filtering ability. Quick to react to their surroundings, oysters offer a useful early warning of pollution in the water or an increase in temperature.

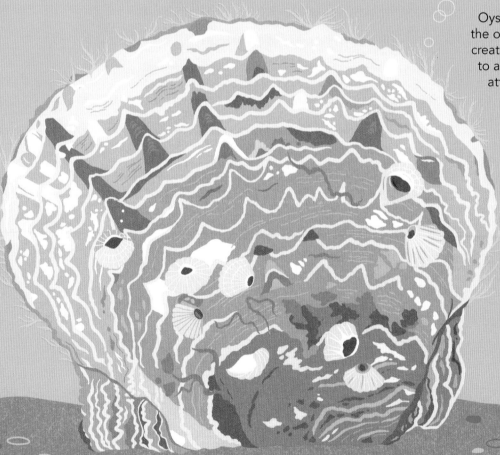

KEY FACTS

Scientific name: *Pinctada maxima*
Size: Diameter: up to 30.5cm
Diet: Phytoplankton
Status: Not evaluated

Amazing fact: Pearls that occur naturally can be irregular and often pear-shaped. Cultured pearls tend to be smoother and more round.

BLUE WHALE

The largest animal on Earth, the magnificent blue whale is also the heaviest-known creature of all time. Some dinosaur skeletons are long enough to rival the blue whale, but we are yet to find evidence of a dinosaur that would have weighed more than this giant of the oceans.

MEALS OF MILLIONS

A blue whale feeding is one of nature's most incredible mealtimes. Sometimes going long periods of time without a meal, blue whales search for large swarms of tiny krill. In the summer, when food is more plentiful, a blue whale will eat 3.6 tonnes (4 tons) of krill or more each day – that's up to 40 million creatures. Taking a huge gulp with its gigantic mouth, the whale filters krill from the water through hundreds of sieve-like plates called baleen.

MARVELS AND MYSTERIES

Despite its incredible size, the blue whale is surprisingly speedy, swimming at up to 48km (30mi) per hour. The male blue whale also has an exceptionally deep voice, communicating with some sounds that are too low for humans to hear. Calls carry for thousands of kilometres through the ocean, and they are becoming lower every year. Scientists do not yet know what is causing the change, but research is under way to find out.

When it comes to the surface for air, the blue whale's blowhole produces a spout of water up to 9m (30ft) high.

Grooves on the blue whale's throat expand to take in vast mouthfuls of water containing krill.

KEY FACTS

Scientific name: *Balaenoptera musculus*
Size: Length: up to 32.6m
Diet: Mostly krill
Status: Endangered (population increasing)

Amazing fact: The blue whale holds the record for the world's biggest baby. A blue whale calf can be as big as 8m long and 3.6 tonnes at birth. An adult can weigh up to 150 tonnes.

HARPOON HARM

Blue whales are found in parts of every ocean except the Arctic. Worldwide, there are only around 10,000–25,000 blue whales left. The invention of a deck-mounted harpoon cannon in the late 19th century meant that whaling ships could take on the largest whale of all, and they killed hundreds of thousands. Blue whales were highly valued for their oil, meat and a range of products made from their body parts. Whaling is now banned, but the remaining population is so small that recovery is slow.

Whale-oil lamp

A diver with a blue whale in the Pacific Ocean near Mexico

SECRETS OF THE GIANTS

With the help of technology, including underwater and aerial photography, we are now uncovering some of the secrets of blue whale behaviour. By fitting tracking tags, scientists can gather months of data about the speed and location of individuals. Shipping companies also use this information, so they can adjust their shipping lanes to avoid hitting whales. Conservation programmes are teaching people about responsible whale-watching and how we can protect their ocean ecosystem.

Attaching a satellite tag to a blue whale

WHAT HAPPENS NEXT?

Humans are thriving on Earth, but around 60 per cent of other primate species are threatened with extinction. The overall rate of animal species dying out in recent years is alarming. By thinking about our actions and making changes for the better, we can all improve the world around us. Read on to discover how much you have learned already, and find out what you can do to help.

WORKING TOGETHER

Experts say that the number of wild animals on Earth has halved in the last 40 years and the losses continue. This is being described as a mass extinction event. Until animals are lost, we often don't understand how important they are. The largest international agreement on wildlife conservation is called CITES. (Convention on International Trade in Endangered Species of Wild Fauna and Flora). This protects more than 30,000 endangered species by controlling any trade that puts them at risk.

DID YOU DISCOVER . . .

Are you an animal expert? See if you know which creatures in this book fit the decriptions below.

• Which slow, tree-dwelling creature has the ability to heal quickly?

• Which is the largest living land mammal?

• Which is the loudest land animal in the world?

• Which animal is our closest living relative?

• Which is the largest living lizard?

• Which animal has the biggest baby?

The answers can be found below. How did you do? Try creating your own quiz based on your favourite creatures from the book.

BE THE SOLUTION

Humans have the power to make changes for the better. Each of us has skills and intelligence that we can use to protect wildlife and give our own species a better future, in harmony with all life on Earth.

Here are 10 ways you can help the planet:

• **Learn** as much as you can about the natural world and how to treat it well

• **Teach** other people what you know and share ideas on how to protect the environment

• **Think** about how you treat animals, and the effects this can have

• **Find out** about wildlife in your area and see which creatures you can spot

• **Join** local conservation groups

• **Follow** environmental news on television, newspapers and magazines

• **Choose** products that do not threaten natural resources or harm the environment

• **Raise** awareness and money for your favourite animal charity or conservation organisation

• **Keep** a wild area in your garden for wildlife, or keep a window box to attract insects

• **Recycle** and re-use as much as you can.

Answers: Maned three-toed sloth, African savannah elephant, Howler monkey, Chimpanzee (and bonobo), Komodo dragon, Blue whale

Pangolins are the most illegally traded mammals in the world. They now have the highest level of protection from CITES.

THE ANIMAL BOOK

AUTHOR
RUTH MARTIN

Ruth has written more than 40 books, for children of all ages. She specialises in non-fiction about wildlife and the natural world.

"My favourite animal in the book is the beautiful Bengal tiger. My hope is that we find lasting ways to protect these species in the wild for future generations to love."

ILLUSTRATOR
DAWN COOPER

Dawn is hugely inspired by the natural world and her work has featured in books, maps, cards and packaging.

"I enjoy taking my camera out on nature walks to gather ideas. My favourite animal in the book is the Maned three-toed sloth, for its laid-back and lovable nature."

DESIGNER
SALLY BOND

Sally has designed illustrated picture books for both adults and children for over 20 years, covering a huge variety of interesting subjects.

"I've always had a fascination with nature and I'm so glad this book has reminded me how truly amazing each and every animal species is. My favourite is the nine-banded armadillo."

Published in September 2017
by Lonely Planet Global Ltd.
CRN 554153
ISBN 978 1 78657 433 6
www.lonelyplanetkids.com
© Lonely Planet 2017

10 9 8 7 6 5 4 3 2 1

Printed in Singapore

Publishing Director Piers Pickard
Publisher and Commissioning Editor Tim Cook
Designer Sally Bond
In-house Senior Designer Andy Mansfield
Illustrator Dawn Cooper
Author Ruth Martin
Zoology consultant Dr Kim Dennis-Bryan
Picture research Sarah Smithies,
Luped Media Research
Editor Catherine Brereton
Print production Larissa Frost and Nigel Longuet

With thanks to
Herman Viola, Native America Consultant

LONELY PLANET OFFICES

AUSTRALIA
The Malt Store, Level 3, 551 Swanston St,
Carlton, Victoria 3053
T: 03 8379 8000

IRELAND
Unit E, Digital Court, The Digital Hub,
Rainsford St, Dublin 8

USA
124 Linden St, Oakland, CA 94607
T: 510 250 6400

UK
240 Blackfriars Rd, London SE1 8NW
T: 020 3771 5100

STAY IN TOUCH lonelyplanet.com/contact

MIX
Paper from
responsible sources
FSC™ C021741

Paper in this book is certified against the Forest Stewardship Council™ standards. FSC™ promotes environmentally responsible, socially beneficial and economically viable management of the world's forests.

GLOSSARY

CARNIVORE An animal that eats meat.

CLIMATE CHANGE A long-term change in the planet's overall temperature, weather patterns or typical conditions.

CONSERVATION Protecting ecosystems and the animals and plants that live in them through organised actions.

CONSERVATIONIST A person who works to protect wildlife and the natural environment.

DEFORESTATION The large-scale removal of trees from forests or woodlands, often caused by human activity such as logging or burning.

DOMESTIC ANIMALS Creatures that live with people and are bred for companionship as pets, or for food, or as working animals.

ECOLOGICALLY EXTINCT When a species is reduced to such low numbers that it no longer has an effect on other species or its environment.

ECOSYSTEM The plants, animals and other organisms that live in a particular environment. An ecosystem also includes non-living things, such as rocks, soil and water.

ECO-TOURISM Travelling to a place to see the natural environment and wildlife in a way that benefits the local community and does not cause damage.

ECTOPARASITE An organism that lives on the outside of another organism, called its host.

ENVIRONMENT The natural surroundings of an animal, plant or other organism, including everything that affects it. The word can be used to describe a tiny area or the whole Earth.

EQUATOR The imaginary line halfway between the North Pole and the South Pole that divides the Earth into two halves called the Northern Hemisphere and the Southern Hemisphere.

EXTINCTION When every single member of a species of animal or plant has died out and no longer exists on Earth.

GLOBAL WARMING A gradual increase in the temperature of Earth's atmosphere, generally due to the greenhouse effect (see GREENHOUSE EFFECT).

GREENHOUSE EFFECT The effect caused by certain gases in Earth's atmosphere that prevent heat escaping. This trapped heat warms Earth's surface. Some human activities, such as burning coal, oil and gas, add to the gases in the atmosphere and increase the greenhouse effect.

HABITAT An area with particular physical and biological features where a plant or animal lives. Examples of habitats include deserts, woodland and forests.

HERBIVORE An animal that eats plants.

ILLEGAL TRADE Buying or selling items against the law, such as protected wildlife or their products.

MIGRATION The movement of an organism from one place to another, usually for food, safety or to breed. The journey may be made many times or just once.

ORGANISM An individual living thing. Organisms include plants, animals, bacteria and fungi.

PARASITE An organism that lives on another organism, called its host. The parasite benefits from this, but the host is harmed and may eventually die.

PESTICIDE Chemicals used to kill pests including weeds, fungi and some insects.

PLANKTON Plankton is a collective word for many small and microscopic organisms that drift freely in marine environments. Plankton forms a vital part of the marine food chain.

POACHING Illegal hunting, killing or capturing of wildlife.

POLLUTION When the environment is damaged or dirtied by harmful substances such as chemicals and waste, nearly always because of humans. There are three main forms of pollution: air, water, and land.

RECYCLING A process that makes used items into new materials and objects.

SMUGGLING Moving goods secretly between countries against the law.

ZOOPLANKTON (See PLANKTON) Zooplankton are animal plankton, while phytoplankton are plankton that can produce energy from sunlight.

INDEX

PICTURE CREDITS

The publisher would like to thank the following for their kind permission to reproduce their photographs:

(Key: a-above; b-below/bottom; c-centre; f-far; l-left; r-right; t-top)

Alamy: Patti McConville 9 (bl); Design Pics Inc/Alaska Stock/Patrick Endres 9 (cla); Chronicle 12 (c); Arco Images GmbH/Therin-Weise 14 (bl); Design Pics Inc/Doug Lindstrand 16 (cr); SuperStock/RGB Ventures/Steven Kazlowski 19 (cr); Paul Brown 20 (ca); Gary Warnimont 22 (cl); Fresh Start Images 24 (br); Jeffrey Thompson 27 (bl); Tom Mareschal 30 (cr); imageBROKER/Dieter Hopf 31 (tl); DanitaDelimont.com/Richard & Susan Day 32 (cl); Buddy Mays 33 (cl); National Geographic Creative/Kike Calvo 33 (bc); USFWS Photo 35 (tl); Brian Bevan 36(cl); Rick & Nora Bowers 37 (tl); DanitaDelimont.com/Pete Oxford 41 (clb); Mark Duffy 41 (tl); Arco/G. Lacz 45 (bl); Laura Romin & Larry Dalton 46 (br); Granger Historical Picture Archive 48 (clb); Arco/G. Lacz 50 (cr); Minden Pictures/Pete Oxford 53 (tl); Christopher Pillitz 54 (tr); Bill Bachmann 56 (cr); Juniors Bildarchiv/F304 59 (bl); Blickwinkel 60 (bl); Ken Welsh 63 (bc); Arterra Picture Library/Raes Johan 63 (tr); Reuters/Marko Djurica 63 (cl); radnorimages 64 (ca); E.D. Torial 66 (br); National Geographic Creativ/Vincent J. Musi 66 (tc); Magica 68 (cl); BonkersAboutScience 71 (tr); Terry Whittaker 71 (cl); Tom Uhlman 72 (cl); blickwinkel/Woike 79 (br); blickwinkel Schmidbauer 80 (tl); Sanjay Shrishrimal 81 (tl); Bruce Coleman Inc/Avalon/Kay & Karl Ammann 82 (tr); Ingo Arndt/Nature Picture Library 85 (cr); Xinhua/Su Yang 87 (br); Krys Bailey 91 (br); Martin Harvey 92 (cl); Steve Bloom Images 94 (tr); EPA/Stephen Morrison 95 (tr); Natural Visions 106 (bl); Hira Punjabi 108 (tr); Robert Harding 110 (l); Reuters/Roger Bacon 114-115 (tc); Louise Murray 115 (cl); ephotocorp/ Avinash Harpude 116 (c); Enrique de la Osa/Reuters 116 (br); Anders Ryman 118 (bl); ZUMA Press, Inc. 121 (br); Reuters/Roger Bacon 126 (br); Boaz Rottem 127 (cr); National Geographic Creative/Joel Sartore 129 (br); Reuters/Stringer Australia 129 (cl); NG Images 130 (bc); Kevin Elsby 137 (bl); Stocktrek Images 138 (cla); Xinhua 138 (ca); imageBROKER/Norbert Eisele-Hein 139 (br); Image Source/Stephen Frink 142 (c); WaterFrame 146 (cla); Jeff Milisen 147 (cla); SuperStock/RGB Ventures/Karen Kasmauski 149 (tr); imageBROKER/Norbert Probst 152 (cl); José Francisco Martín Piñatel 153 (tl); Jeremy Sutton-Hibbert 155 (bc); Minden Pictures/Flip Nicklin 159 (clb); Minden Pictures/Norbert Wu 159 (cla). **ARC-PIC.COM:** Carsten Egevang 16 (clb). **ArcticPhoto:** B&C Alexander 10 (cl). **ardea.com:** Tom & Pat Leeson 21 (cl); Biosphoto/Quentin Martinez 44 (tl); Auscape 134 (cb). **AWL Images:** Alex Robinson 38 (br); Nigel Pavitt 76 (b);); Nordic Photos 100 (l); Jonathan & Angela Scott 130 (bl). **Shelley Banks** 32 (br). **Bridgeman Images:** Peabody Essex Museum, Salem, Massachusetts, USA 29 (c); Bibliotheque Nationale, Paris, France 67 (tl); State Hermitage Museum, St. Petersburg, Russia 70 (br). **CGTrader** 11 (br). **Kester Clarke** 39 (tl). **FLPA:** Minden Pictures/Flip

Nicklin 13 (cr); Minden Pictures/Michael Quinton 16 (bl); Minden Pictures/Flip Nicklin 17 (crb); Minden Pictures/Ingo Arndt 35 (cr); Minden Pictures/Michael & Patricia Fogden 47 (tl); Minden Pictures/ZSSD 48 (bc); Minden Pictures/Luciano Candisani 49 (tl); Minden Pictures/Luciano Candisani 55 (cl); Minden Pictures/Suzi Eszterhas 55 (tr); Minden Pictures/Luciano Candisani 55 (bl); Minden Pictures/Ernst Dirksen, Buiten-beeld 59 (tl); Minden Pictures/Pete Oxford 64 (br); Minden Pictures/ZSSD 79 (tr); Minden Pictures/Jan van der Greef 83 (cb); Biosphoto/Theo Allofs 91 (cb); Chris Mattison 99 (cr); Biosphoto/Olivier Born 117 (br); Biosphoto/Olivier Born 117 (cb); Minden Pictures/Mark Jones 119 (tl); Minden Pictures/Colin Monteath 124 (tc); Neil Bowman 125 (cl); Minden Pictures/Suzi Eszterhas 129 (tr); Minden Pictures/Suzi Eszterhas 133 (br); Minden Pictures/Pete Oxford 133 (cla); Minden Pictures/Pete Oxford 133 (tr); Minden Pictures/Stefan Christmann 134 (clb); Biosphoto/Samuel Blanc 134 (tr); Minden Pictures/Richard Herrmann 137 (tl); Minden Pictures/Flip Nicklin 137 (crb); D P Wilson 143 (ca); Minden Pictures/Flip Nicklin 144 (cl); Malcolm Schuyl 144 (cr); Frans Lanting 145 (cl); D P Wilson 146 (bl); Photo Researchers 151 (cl); Frans Lanting 156 (bc); Steve Trewhella 156 (tr). **Jan van Franeker** Wageningen Marine Research 17 (ca). **Getty Images:** Robert Harding/Louise Murray 8 (tl); Corbis/In Pictures Ltd/Barry Lewis 8 (bc); E+/RyersonClark 8 (bl); Corbis Historical/George Rinhart 9 (br); National Geographic/Brian J. Skerry 12 (cl); National Geographic/Ralph Lee Hopkins 15 (bl); National Geographic/Paul Nicklen 19 (tl); iStock/rypson 20 (cra); Universal Images Group/AGF 20 (clb); EyeEm/Yoshie Kimura 20 (bl); Robert Harding/Gary Cook 21 (br); Underwood Archives 23 (cr); Corbis/VCG/Tim Davis 23 (tc); Corbis/William Campbell 23 (tl); TNS/Wichita Eagle/Bo Rader 24 (cl); National Geographic/Steve Winter 25 (bl); Photolibrary/Michelle McCarron 25 (ca); National Geographic/George Grall 26 (c); First Light/Thomas Kitchin & Victoria Hurst 27 (tr); Moment/David C Stephens 27 (tl); iStock/JREden 28-29 (tc); Corbis Documentary/Joel Rogers 30 (ca); Moment/Dagny Willis 30 (tl); Photographer's Choice/Friedrich Schmidt 31 (bl); E+/stanley45 34 (cl); iStock/rainbow-7 35 (cl); Gallo Images/Danita Delimont 36 (cr); Moment/Kelly Cheng Travel Photography 38 (cl); Franck Chaput/Hemis.fr 118 (bl) Photographer's Choice/Tim Thompson 38 (bl); De Agostini/A. Curzi 39 (bl); Robert Harding/Mick Baines & Maren Reichelt 39 (br); National Geographic/Bianca Lavies 40 c; National Geographic/Bianca Lavies 40 (tr); Dorling Kindersley 40 (cl); Franco Banfi 43 (tr); Science Source/Simon D Pollard 44 c; Photolibrary/Timothy Allen 44 (bl); Oxford Scientific/Mark Jones Roving Tortoise Photos 45 (tc); Panoramic Images 46 (tl); Panoramic Images 46 (bl); Corbis/Fuse 48 (tl); Wim van den Heever 48 (cla); Stone/Tim Flach 49 (cr)a; Dinodia Photo/Passage 49 (crb); National Geographic/Bill Hatcher 50 (bl); Mint Images/Frans Lanting 51 (tl); Bettmann 52 (ca); STF/Gabriel Rossi 54 (cl); LightRocket/Fotoholica Press 54 (cr); Moment/Sysaworld/Roberto

Moiola 56 (cl); Corbis Documentary/Roger Hosking 57 (c); Hemera/S. Te strake 58 (tr); AFP/Stringer 58 (bl); Corbis Historical/Hulton Deutsch 58 (cr); Nature Picture Library/Angelo Gandolfi 61 (tl); Science Photo Library/Dr Jeremy Burgess 68 (br); SPL (cr)eative/Harmer Andy 70 (tl); Biosphoto/Michel Gunther 70 (cl); Sean Gallup 71 (bl); Photolibrary/Stephen Shepherd 72 (br); AFP/Leon Neal 73 (tl); Westend61 74 (tl); iStock/stocksnapper 74 (ca); SPL/K.H. Kjeldsen 75 (tr); Photographer's Choice/Tom Bonaventure 76 (tr); E+/Bartosz Hadyniak 76 (cl); Richard du Toit/Gallo Images 77 (cl); Richard du Toit/Gallo Images 78 (cl); E+/brittak 81 (cr); markrhiggins 82 (cla); Corbis Documentary/Gallo Images 82 (cr); iStock/BirdImages 83 (cr); javarman3/iStock 84 (tr); Mike Powles/Oxford Scientific 88 (br); Stockbyte 88 (cl); Gallo Images 90 (tl); Konrad Wothe 93 (bl); DeAgostini 95 (cla); Sia Kambou/AFP 95 (cl); Claudia Uribe/Photodisc 97 (tl); Volanthevist/Moment 97 (br); NurPhoto 100 (br); Visuals Unlimited, Inc./Thomas Marent 101 (br); Andy Rouse/The Image Bank 102 (tl); Nigel Pavitt/AWL Images 102 (tr); Catherine Leblanc/Corbis Documentary 103 (tr); AYImages/E+ 105 (tl); Juni Kriswanto/AFP 105 (cla); VCG 107 (bc); Dinodia Photo 108 (br); Robert Nickelsberg 109 (bc); iStock/kajornyot 109 (tr); Snow Leopard Trust And NCF/Barcroft India 112 (cr); Snow Leopard Trust And NCF/Barcroft India 112 (tr); Tuul and Bruno Morandi/Photolibrary 113 (tc); National Geographic/Steve Winter 115 (cr); Oxford Scientific/David Maitland 116 (cra); Hannah Peters 119 (c); Corbis Documentary/Jami Tarris 120 (bl); Universal Images Group/Auscape 120 (ca); imageBROKER/jspix 121 (cl); National Geographic/Jason Edwards 122 (cla); AFP/Torsten Blackwood 122 (bl); National Geographic/Medford Taylor 123 (bl); Photolibrary/Andrew Roesler 124 (tl); Handout 124 (bl); National Geographic/Lynn Johnson 125 (cbl); Stringer/David Hardenberg 125 (cr); Universal Images Group/Auscape 126 (ca); Adam Pretty 127 (bc); John White Photos 129 (bc); All Canada Photos/Wayne Lynch 131 (crb); Theo Allofs 131 (ca); Mint Images/Frans Lanting 134 (br); Corbis/VCG/DLILLC 134 (c); All Canada Photos/Wayne Lynch 136 (cl); Moment Mobile/Schafer & Hill 137 (cra); The Boston Globe/Wendy Maeda 141 (ca); Moment/Stoneography 142 (cr); WaterFrame/Daniela Dirscherl 142 (tl); Oxford Scientific/Rodger Jackman 143 (tr); The Asahi Shimbun 144 (br); Corbis/Timothy Fadek 145 (tl); Science Photo Library/Volker Steger 147 (tr); National Geographic/Marc Moritsch 148 (cra); Oxford Scientific/David Courtenay 148 (cl); ullstein bild/Reinhard Dirscherl 151 (br); Nature Picture Library/Jurgen Freund 152 (tl); Biosphoto/Sergi Garcia Fernandez 154 (tl); ullstein bild/Reinhard Dirscherl 155 (cl); Nature Picture Library/Jurgen Freund 157 (tl); Photolibrary/Mark Carwardine 159 (crb); Science & Society Picture Library 159 (tc). **Lonely Planet Images:** Martin Moos 61 (cla); Jean-Pierre Lescourret 56 (br); Manfred Gottschalk 53 (br); Matt Munro 74 (cr); travelgame 118 (cr). **National Library of New Zealand** Michael Collett 74 (br). **Nature Picture Library:** Bryan and Cherry Alexander 11

(tr); Jurgen Freund 12 (cr); Bryan & Cherry Alexander 13 (cla); Sue Flood 14 (br); Rolf Nussbaumer 26 (cl); Rolf Nussbaumer 26 (tr); ARCO 27 (cl); Doug Wechsler 36 (bl); Juan Manuel Borrero 36 (bc); Mark Bowler 42 (cl); Francois Savigny 43 (br); Jim Clare 47 (bl); Nick Upton 47 cb; Roland Seitre 50 (crb); Dave Bevan 57 (cr); Warwick Sloss 60 (cr); Laurie Campbell 61 (clb); Klaus Echle 62 (tr); Tom Marshall 65 (cl); Ernie Janes 66 (cr); Roland Seitre 67 (bl); David Pattyn 72 (tr); Stephen Dalton 75 (tl); Constantinos Petrinos 78 (cl); Yuri Shibnev 84 (cr)a; Stephen Dalton 85 (bc); Anup Shah 87 (tc); Anup Shah 87 (cl); Ann & Steve Toon 88 (cb); Richard Du Toit 89 (br); Ashish & Shanthi Chandola 89 (tl); Richard Du Toit 89 (ca); David Pattyn 93 (cla); Eric Baccega 94 (br); Christophe Couteau 94 (ca); Inaki Relanzon 96 t; Anup Shah 96 (c); Bernard Castelein 96 (crb); Edwin Giesbers 98 (br); Barrie Britton 98 (cl); Alex Hyde 99 (tc); Juan Carlos Munoz 101 (cl); Suzi Eszterhas 101 (tl); Tony Heald 102 (bc); Michael Pitts 105 (crb); Gavin Maxwell 107 (tl); Aflo 111 (tr); Eric Dragesco 112 (cl); Sandesh Kadur 117 (bl); Sandesh Kadur 117 (tr); Visuals Unlimited 122 (cr); Miles Barton 123 (tl); Dave Watts 126 (cr); Roland Seitre 127 (cl); Roland Seitre 129 (tl); Kathryn Jeffs 131 (tl); Juan Carlos Munoz 132 (crb); Mike Read 132 (bl); Pete Oxford 133 (clb); Roy Mangersnes 136 (bl); Gabriel Rojo 136 (cr); Dan Burton 139 cb; Doc White 140 (tc); Claudio Contreras 141 (bl); Chris & Monique Fallows 141 (tr); Doug Wechsler 145 (cr); Solvin Zankl 150 (tl); Alex Mustard 151 (bl); Jurgen Freund 154 (br); Doug Perrine 154 (tr); Jurgen Freund 157 (cra); Doc White 158 (tr); Edwin Giesbers 98-99 (tc). **Oceanwideimages.com** Rudie Kuiter 139 (tr). **PA Images:** Associated Press 25 (br); PA Images / Associated Press/Kamran Jebreili 111 (bl); Associated Press/Koji Sasahara 156 (cla). **Photoshot:** NHPA/Vincent Gesser 7 (c); NHPA/Laurie Campbell 65 (tl); NHPA/William Paton 67 (tr); NHPA/Hellio & Van Ingen 85 (cla); NHPA/Photo Researchers 104 (bl). **Project Gutenberg** 65 (tr). **QUT** Richard Fitzpatrick 143 (clb). **Rex/Shutterstock** KeystoneUSA-ZUMA 18 (cl); AeroVironment Inc. 32 (bc); Sipa Press 107 (cr); EPA/Carl Whetham 113 (br). **Science Photo Library:** Philippe Psaila 69 (tl); Volker Steger 147 (cla). **Shutterstock:** vector graphics 6 (br); Vladimir Melnikov 11 (ca); Helen Birkin 15 (crb); Richard Laschon 24 (tr); Todd Klassy 29 (tr); Maria Jeffs 33 (tl); Deatonphotos 37 (cra); chamleunejai 42 (bl); Miroslav Hlavko 57 (bc); Will Howe 59 (cb); Michal Ninger 60 (bl); Cherry-Merry 62 (cr); Steve Oehlenschlager 69 (tr); Michael Taylor 75 (bl); bikeriderlondon 77 (bl); Sergey Uryadnikov 77 (tl); Stephanie Periquet 78 (ca); Dennis Jacobsen 79 (bl); Pius Lee 80 (bl); Gudkov Andrey 83 (tr); Sergey Uryadnikov 86 (tr); Daria Volyanskaya 90 (cr)a; Vladimir Wrangel 91 (tc); Kongsak Sumano 93 (cr); AgriTech 109 (br); PeterVrabel 110 (tr); Alfonso de Tomas 130 (tr); Jordan Tan 150 (tr); JGA 153 (cra). **Superstock** Wild Nature Photos 37 (cl). **Eric Warrant** 90 (cb). **Wildlife Conservation Society** 29 (br).